MENSA®

THE HIGH IQ SOCIETY

LOGIC
BRAINTEASERS

THIS IS A CARLTON BOOK

Text and puzzle content copyright © British Mensa Limited 1996, 2006
Design and artwork copyright © Carlton Books Limited 1996, 2006

This edition published by Carlton Books Limited 2006
20 Mortimer Street
London W1T 3JW

A CIP catalogue for this book is available from the British Library.

ISBN 978-1-84442-338-5

Printed in Great Britain

MENSA
THE HIGH IQ SOCIETY

LOGIC
BRAINTEASERS

Philip Carter & Ken Russell

CARLTON

INTRODUCTION

People often feel that there's something a bit cold about logic. It reminds us of Mr Spock playing multidimensional chess, his mighty Vulcan brain remorselessly analysing every possible permutation of the game. Even worse, it makes us think about mathematics lessons where we sweated over some ghastly geometric conundrum that stubbornly refused to yield up its dusty secrets. Fortunately, it does not have to be that way.

Ken Russell and Philip Carter, who for many years have been Mensa's resident puzzle experts, have come up with a collection of logic puzzles just for fun. The nice thing about logic is that it does not require any special knowledge, just a capacity for following an argument one step at a time to its inevitable conclusion. There is something extremely satisfying in being able to take a knotty problem and, after having carefully unpicked the complications, arriving at the solution.

R. P. Allen

Robert Allen

Mensa is the international society for people with a high IQ.
We have more than 100,000 members in over 40 countries worldwide.

The society's aims are:
> to identify and foster human intelligence for the benefit of humanity
> to encourage research in the nature, characteristics, and uses of intelligence
> to provide a stimulating intellectual and social environment for its members

Anyone with an IQ score in the top two per cent of population is eligible to become a member of Mensa – are you the 'one in 50' we've been looking for?

Mensa membership offers an excellent range of benefits:
> Networking and social activities nationally and around the world
> Special Interest Groups – hundreds of chances to pursue your hobbies and interests – from art to zoology!
> Monthly members' magazine and regional newsletters
> Local meetings – from games challenges to food and drink
> National and international weekend gatherings and conferences
> Intellectually stimulating lectures and seminars
> Access to the worldwide SIGHT network for travellers and hosts

For more information about Mensa: www.mensa.org, or

British Mensa Ltd.,
St John's House,
St John's Square,
Wolverhampton
WV2 4AH
Telephone: +44 (0) 1902 772771
E-mail: enquiries@mensa.org.uk
www.mensa.org.uk

Dazzling Diamond

Divide the diamond into four identical shapes, each containing one of each of the following five symbols:

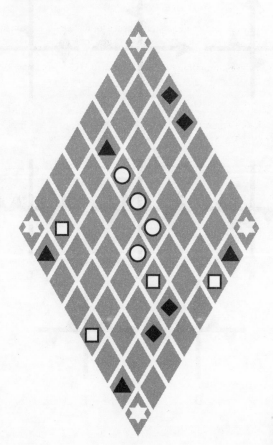

see answer
21

Look at the three shapes. Does option A, B, C, D or E continue the sequence?

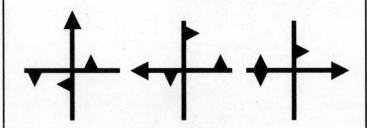

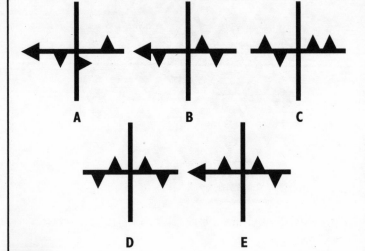

A   B   C

D   E

see answer
5

Roving Robot

Scientists have produced a robot that contains a simple program for crossing a quiet road (not a one-way street) in the UK.

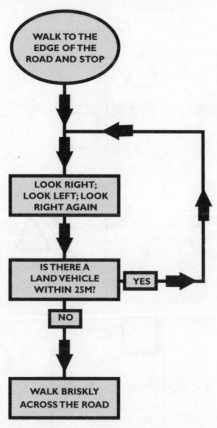

WALK TO THE EDGE OF THE ROAD AND STOP

LOOK RIGHT; LOOK LEFT; LOOK RIGHT AGAIN

IS THERE A LAND VEHICLE WITHIN 25M?

YES

NO

WALK BRISKLY ACROSS THE ROAD

But they made a cardinal error and the robot takes eight hours to cross the road. What is the error?

see answer
20

Three Circles

Draw three complete circles so that each contains one ellipse, one square and one triangle. No two circles may use all the same elements.

see answer
2

Counterfeit Coins

Most counterfeit coin puzzles assume you have balance-type scales available with two pans, where one object is weighed against another. In this puzzle you have a single scale with only one pan. You have three bags of large gold coins with an unspecified number of coins in each bag. One of the bags consists entirely of counterfeit coins weighing 55g each; the other two bags contain all genuine coins weighing 50g each.

What is the minimum number of weighing operations you need to carry out before you can be certain of identifying the bag of counterfeit coins?

see answer
15

At this school the boys sit at desks numbered 1–5 and the girls sit opposite them at desks numbered 6–10.

1. The girl sitting next to the girl opposite desk number 1 is Fiona.
2. Fiona is three desks away from Grace.
3. Hilary is opposite Colin.
4. Eddy is opposite the girl next to Hilary.
5. If Colin is not central then Alan is.
6. David is next to Bill.
7. Bill is three desks away from Colin.
8. If Fiona is not central then Indira is.
9. Hilary is three desks away from Jane.
10. David is opposite Grace.
11. The girl sitting next to the girl opposite Alan is Jane.
12. Colin is not at desk number 5.
13. Jane is not at desk number 10.

Can you work out the seating arrangements?

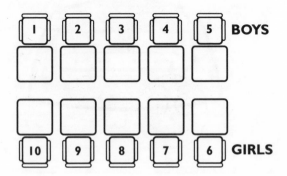

see answer
16

Making Eyes

Look at the five drawings. Does A, B, C, D or E continue the sequence?

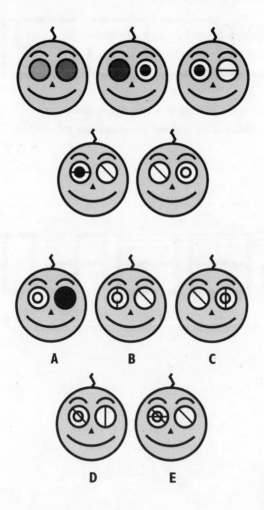

A B C

D E

see answer
13

Look at the five figures above.
Which of the following options continues the sequence?

A   B   C   D   E

see answer
17

Converging Circles

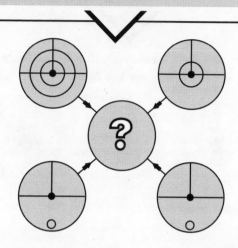

Each line and symbol in the four outer circles is transferred to the middle circle according to a few rules. These are that if a line or symbol occurs in the outer circles:

once, it is transferred; twice, it is possibly transferred; three times, it is transferred; four times, it is not transferred.

Which of the five circles should appear in the middle of the diagram above?

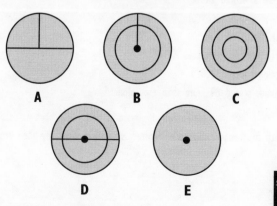

see answer
10

Shooting Range

Three military marksmen — Colonel Present, Major Aim and General Fire — are shooting on the range. When they have finished, they collect their targets.

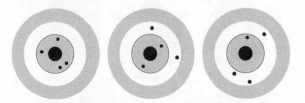

Each makes three statements:

Colonel Present:
"I scored 180."
"I scored 40 less than the major."
"I scored 20 more than the general."

Major Aim:
"I did not score the lowest."
"The difference between my score and the general's was 60."
"The general scored 240."

General Fire:
"I scored less than the colonel."
"The colonel scored 200."
"The major scored 60 more than the colonel."

Each marksman makes one incorrect statement. What are their scores?

see answer
14

In the land of Zoz there live three types of person:

Truthkins, who live in hexagonal houses and always tell the truth;
Fibkins, who live in pentagonal houses and always tell lies;
Switchkins, who live in round houses and who make true whatever they say.

One morning 90 of them gather in the city in three groups of 30. One group is all of one type; another group is made up evenly of two types; the third group evenly comprises three types. Everyone in the first group says "We are all truthkins"; everyone in the second group says "We are all fibkins"; and everyone in the third group says "We are all switchkins".

How many sleep in pentagonal houses that night?

see answer
12

Fancy Figures

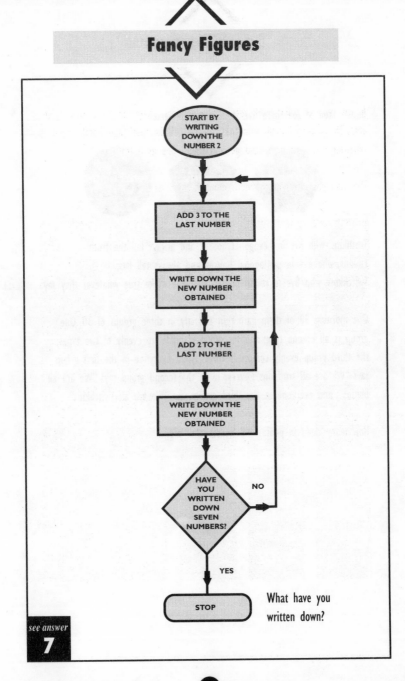

START BY WRITING DOWN THE NUMBER 2

ADD 3 TO THE LAST NUMBER

WRITE DOWN THE NEW NUMBER OBTAINED

ADD 2 TO THE LAST NUMBER

WRITE DOWN THE NEW NUMBER OBTAINED

HAVE YOU WRITTEN DOWN SEVEN NUMBERS?

NO

YES

STOP

What have you written down?

see answer 7

Booth Bonanza

A new repairer starts work repairing telephones. There are 15 booths in his area. The supervisor tells him that five out of the first eight booths need repairing and that he should go and repair one as a test.

The man goes straight to booth number eight. Why?

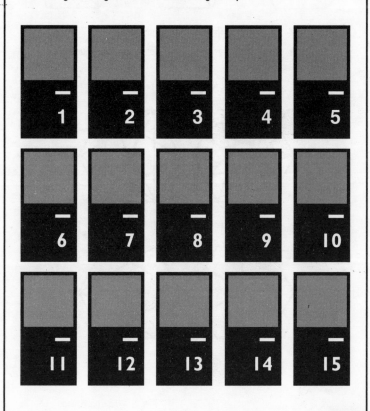

see answer
4

Hexagon Harmony

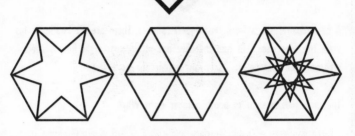

Look at the three hexagons above.
Which of the following four options continues the sequence?

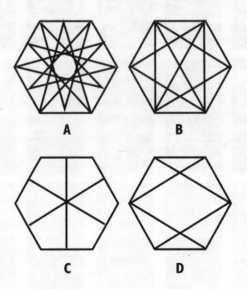

A

B

C

D

see answer
8

Three gamblers — Diablo, Scarface and Lucky — attend a convention at Las Vegas. They decide to have a gambling session with six-sided dice, but stipulate unusual rules:

1. Each gambler may select his own numbers.
2. The numbers 1–9 may be selected, but no two numbers may be consecutive.
3. Each die has to have three pairs of different numbers, adding up to 30.

In addition, no two gamblers are allowed to choose the same combination of numbers. In a long run, Diablo's numbers will beat Scarface; Scarface's numbers will beat Lucky; but Lucky's numbers will beat Diablo. How is this possible?

see answer
1

Four suspects — Jack Vicious, Sid Shifty, Alf Muggins and Jim Pouncer — are being interviewed at the scene of a murder. Each of the suspects is asked a question. Their answers are as follows:

Jack Vicious: "Sid Shifty committed the murder."
Sid Shifty: "Jim Pouncer committed the murder."
Alf Muggins: "I didn't commit the murder."
Jim Pouncer: "Sid Shifty is lying."

Only one of the four answers is the truth. Who committed the murder?

see answer
6

Dynamic Dog

Russell Carter lives on a remote ranch in the Australian outback with his dog, Spot. Several times a week he sets off with Spot for a long walk. This morning he is walking at a steady 4mph. When they are 10 miles from home Russell turns to walk back and, retracing his steps, lets Spot off the lead. The dog immediately runs homeward at 9mph. When Spot reaches the ranch he turns around and runs back to Russell, who is continuing at his steady 4mph. On reaching Russell, Spot turns back for the ranch, maintaining his 9mph. This is repeated until Russell arrives back at the ranch and lets Spot in. At all times Russell and Spot maintain their respective speeds of 4mph and 9mph.

How many miles does Spot cover from being let off the lead to being let into the ranch?

see answer
19

Manor House

In the English countryside is a traditional manor house. Five staff work there, each of whom has a different hobby and a different rest day.

		OCCUPATION					PASTIME					REST DAY				
		BUTLER	CHAUFFEUR	COOK	GARDENER	JANITOR	FISHING	CHESS	SQUASH	BRIDGE	GOLF	MONDAY	TUESDAY	WEDNESDAY	THURSDAY	FRIDAY
NAME	SMITH															
	JONES															
	WOOD															
	CLARK															
	JAMES															
REST DAY	MONDAY															
	TUESDAY															
	WEDNESDAY															
	THURSDAY															
	FRIDAY															
PASTIME	FISHING															
	CHESS															
	SQUASH															
	BRIDGE															
	GOLF															

1. The man who has Tuesdays off plays golf but is not the janitor, who is called Clark.

2. Jones is not the butler who plays squash.

3. Wood has Wednesdays off and is not the butler or the gardener.

4. James is the cook and does not have Thursdays off; Smith also does not have Thursdays off.

5. Bridge is played on Mondays; the chauffeur does not play chess; and James does not have Tuesdays off.

What are their names, how is each employed, what is the pastime of each, and on which day of the week does each have a rest day?

NAME	OCCUPATION	PASTIME	REST DAY

see answer

9

House Hunting

My friend, Archibald, has moved into a new house in a long road in which the houses are numbered consecutively, 1–82. To find out his house number I ask him three questions to which I receive a yes/no answer. I will not tell you the answers, but if you can work them out you will discover his house number. The questions are:

1. Is it under 41?
2. Is it divisible by 4?
3. Is it a square number?

Can you work out the number of Archibald's house?

see answer
18

From my window I can see the town clock. Every day I check the clock on my mantlepiece against the time shown on the town clock. It usually agrees, but one morning a strange situation occurred. My mantlepiece clock showed the time as 5 minutes to 9 o'clock; a minute later it read 4 minutes to 9 o'clock; 2 minutes later it read 4 minutes to 9 o'clock; a minute later it read 5 minutes to 9 o'clock.

At 9 o'clock I suddenly realised what was wrong.
Can you tell what it was?

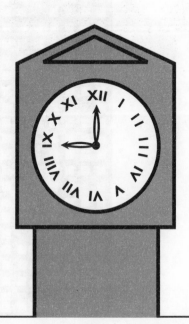

see answer
3

Sears Tower

The national headquarters of Sears Roebuck & Co. in Chicago, Illinois, is the tallest inhabited building in the world. Better known as Sears Tower, it is 225m high plus half its height again.

How high is Sears Tower?

see answer
11

In a hotel in Nagasaki is a glass door. On the door it says:

PHUƧLULꟼ

What does it mean?

see answer
22

Prisoners' Porridge

A jailer has a large number of prisoners to guard and has to seat them at a number of tables at mealtimes. The regulations state the following seating arrangements:

1. Each table is to seat the same number of prisoners.
2. The number at each table is to be an odd number.

The jailer finds that when he seats the prisoners:
3 per table, he has 2 prisoners left over;
5 per table, he has 4 prisoners left over;
7 per table, he has 6 prisoners left over;
9 per table, he has 8 prisoners left over;
but when he seats them 11 per table there are none left over.

How many prisoners are there?

see answer
34

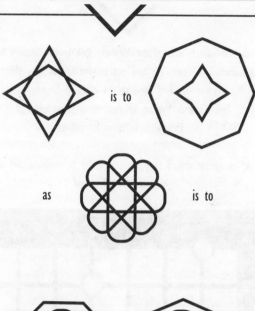

is to

as

is to

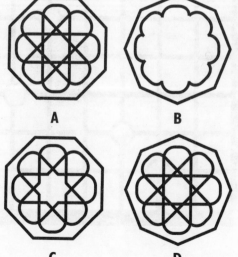

A

B

C

D

see answer
25

Algarve Rendezvous

On the far eastern side of the Algarve, close to the Spanish border, is a town whose roads are laid out in grid fashion, like Manhattan. This system was first used in the cities of Ancient Greece. Seven friends live at different corners, marked ◯. They wish to meet for coffee.

On which corner should they meet in order to minimise the walking distance for all seven?

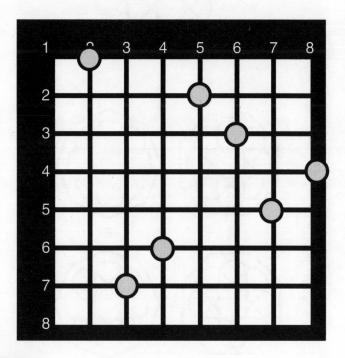

see answer
31

Creative Circles

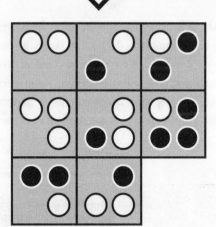

Look along each line and down each column of the shape above.
Which of the following eight options is the missing square?

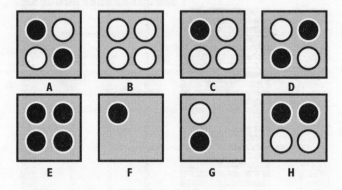

see answer
35

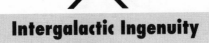

Five pairs of husband and wife aliens arrive for an intergalactic meeting on Earth. For ease of recognition, the males are known by the letter M followed by an odd number and the females by F and an even number. Each pair has different distinguishing features and has prepared a different subject for discussion. They arrive in different types of spacecraft and dock in a set of five bays. The pairs sit in five double seats in the auditorium.

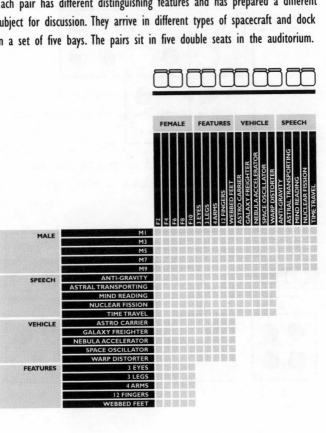

		F2	F4	F6	F8	F10	3 EYES	3 LEGS	4 ARMS	12 FINGERS	WEBBED FEET	ASTRO CARRIER	GALAXY FREIGHTER	NEBULA ACCELERATOR	SPACE OSCILLATOR	WARP DISTORTER	ANTI-GRAVITY	ASTRAL TRANSPORTING	MIND READING	NUCLEAR FISSION	TIME TRAVEL
MALE	M1																				
	M3																				
	M5																				
	M7																				
	M9																				
SPEECH	ANTI-GRAVITY																				
	ASTRAL TRANSPORTING																				
	MIND READING																				
	NUCLEAR FISSION																				
	TIME TRAVEL																				
VEHICLE	ASTRO CARRIER																				
	GALAXY FREIGHTER																				
	NEBULA ACCELERATOR																				
	SPACE OSCILLATOR																				
	WARP DISTORTER																				
FEATURES	3 EYES																				
	3 LEGS																				
	4 ARMS																				
	12 FINGERS																				
	WEBBED FEET																				

Table headers (top): FEMALE, FEATURES, VEHICLE, SPEECH

1. M1 is preparing his speech on time travel and has arrived in a warp distorter.

2. The mind-reading couple, who have four arms each, have parked their nebula accelerator between the space oscillator and the astro carrier.

3. F6, in the seat next to the left-end pair, says to the alien next to her, "My husband, M3, and I have noticed that you have three legs."

4. F4 admires the galaxy freighter owned by the pair who each have three eyes, who are in the next seats.

5. The husband of F8 is turning his papers on time travel with 12 fingers.

6. M5, in the middle pair of seats, says to F10 in the next pair of seats, "The pair with webbed feet on your other side have an astro carrier."

7. M7 and F2 are studying their papers on anti-gravity. The husband of F6 is studying his papers on nuclear fission.

Who is the wife of M9 and who is the male speaker on nuclear fission?

MALE/FEMALE									
SPEECH									
VEHICLE									
FEATURES									

see answer
29

Searching Segments

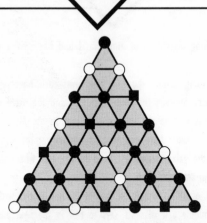

Place the 12 segment links below over the triangular grid in such a way
that each link symbol on the grid is covered by an identical symbol.
The connecting segments must not be rotated. Not all the connecting lines
will be covered.

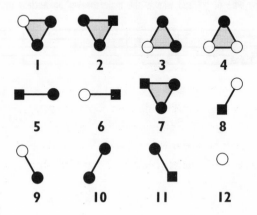

see answer
32

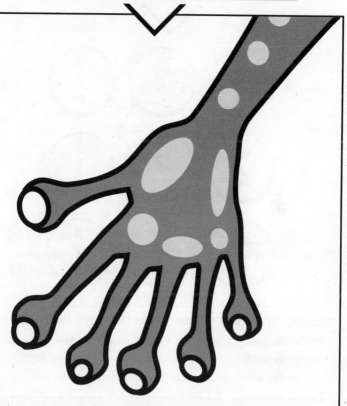

A number of aliens (more than one) are in a room. Each alien has more than one finger on each hand. All the aliens have the same number of fingers as each other and a different number of fingers on each hand. If you knew the total number of fingers in the room you would know how many aliens there were. There are between 200 and 300 alien fingers in the room.

How many aliens are there?

see answer
24

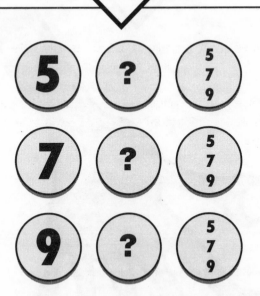

Anastasia has thought of a number between 99 and 999. Belinda asks whether the number is below 500; Anastasia answers yes. Belinda asks whether the number is a square number; Anastasia answers yes. Belinda asks whether the number is a cube number; Anastasia answers yes. However, Anastasia has told the truth to only two of the three questions. Anastasia then tells Belinda truthfully that both the first and the last digit are 5, 7 or 9.

What is the number?

see answer
36

Girl Talk

A census-taker calls at a house. He asks the woman living there the ages of her three daughters.

The woman says, "If you multiply their ages the total is 72; if you add together their ages the total is the same as the number on my front door, which you can see."

The census-taker says, "That is not enough information for me to calculate their ages."

The woman says, "Well, my eldest daughter has a cat with a wooden leg."

The census-taker replies, "Ah! Now I know their ages."

What are the ages of the three girls?

see answer

42

Treasured Trees

Local sports clubs take turns to plant a tree each year in the town's main street. A bird has established a nest in each tree.

1. The crow lives in the beech tree.
2. The lime was planted two years after the tree planted by the golf club.
3. The robin is in the tree planted by the bowling club, which is next to the tree planted by the soccer club.
4. Jim planted his tree in 1971.
5. The starling is in the poplar tree planted by Desmond in 1974.
6. The robin lives in the tree planted by the bowling club, which is next to the tree planted by the soccer club.
7. Tony planted the middle tree — a beech.
8. Bill has an owl in his tree, which is next to the ash.
9. The tree at the right-hand end was planted in 1974 by the soccer club.
10. The elm was planted in 1970.
11. The tennis club planted in 1972.
12. The squash club planted in 1970.
13. Sylvester planted his tree in 1973 and it has a robin in it.
14. The blackbird is in the tree planted by Jim.

TREE				
PERSON				
CLUB				
BIRD				
YEAR				

Work out which tree was planted by which member
of each club and in which year.

see answer
28

There are 189 members of the tennis club:
8 have been at the club less than three years;
11 are under 20 years of age; 70 wear spectacles; 140 are men.

What is the smallest number of players who had been members for three years or more, were at least 20 years of age, wore glasses and were men?

see answer
38

Tree Teaser

Don and Spencer are engaged by the local council to prune trees on either side of a tree-lined avenue. There is an equal number of trees on either side of the road. Don arrives first and has pruned three trees on the right-hand side when Spencer arrives and points out that Don should be pruning the trees on the left-hand side. So Don starts afresh on the left-hand side and Spencer continues on the right. When Spencer has finished his side he crosses the avenue and prunes six trees for Don, which finishes the job.

Who prunes the most trees and by how many?

see answer
41

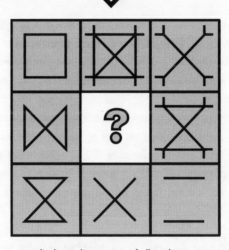

Look at the pattern of tiles above.
Which of the following tiles replaces the question mark?

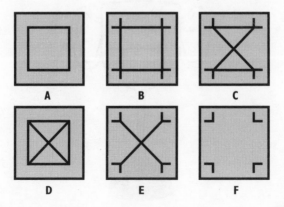

A   B   C

D   E   F

see answer
33

43

There is a somewhat confusing situation at the dog show this year. Four brothers — Andy, Bill, Colin and Donald — each enter two dogs, and each has named his dogs after two of his brothers. Consequently, there are two dogs named Andy, two named Bill, two named Colin and two named Donald.

Of the eight dogs, three are corgis, three labradors and two dalmatians. None of the four brothers owns two dogs of the same breed. No two dogs of the same breed have the same name. Neither of Andy's dogs is named Donald and neither of Colin's dogs is named Andy. No corgi is named Andy and no labrador is named Donald. Bill does not own a labrador.

Who are the owners of the dalmatians and what are the dalmatians' names?

see answer
37

Charlie throws out a challenge to Ben in the local bar: "I'll put this ordinary pocket handkerchief on the floor. You stand facing me on one corner and I'll stand on the other corner. Without either of us tearing, cutting, stretching or altering it in any way, I bet you won't be able to touch me."

How can this be done?

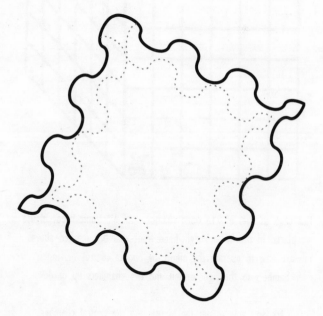

see answer
30

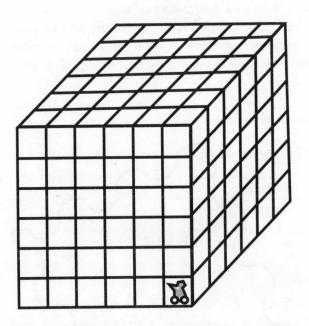

This cage consists of 216 open chambers. An electronic robot mouse is placed in the bottom right-hand front chamber, marked above. You are able to operate the mouse by remote control, moving it three chambers to the right or left and two chambers up or down.

Are you able to get the mouse into the central chamber, and if so, what is the minimum number of moves by which this can be achieved?

see answer
27

46

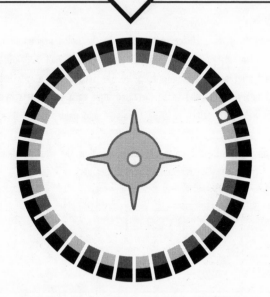

A roulette wheel shows the numbers 1–36. My ball has landed on a particular number that I bet on. It is divisible by 3. When the digits are added together, the total lies between 4 and 8. It is an odd number. When the digits are multiplied together, the total lies between 4 and 8.

Which number have I bet on?

see answer
40

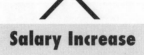

Salary Increase

A company gives a choice of two plans to the union negotiator for an increase in salary. The first option is an initial salary of $20,000 to be increased after each 12 months by $500. The second option is a half-yearly initial salary of $10,000 to be increased after each six months by $125. This half-yearly salary is to be calculated and paid over six months.

Can you advise the union negotiator which is the plan he should recommend to his members?

see answer
23

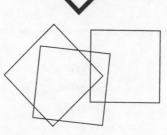

Look at the group of three squares above. They have a certain feature which is shared by only one of the groups of three squares below. What is it, and which group matches?

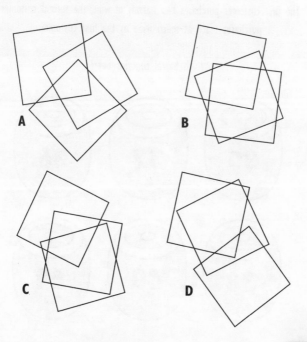

A

B

C

D

see answer
39

A wine merchant has six barrels of wine and beer containing:

30 gallons

32 gallons

36 gallons

38 gallons

40 gallons

62 gallons

Five barrels are filled with wine and one with beer.
The first customer purchases two barrels of wine; the second customer
purchases twice as much wine as the first customer.

Which barrel contains beer?

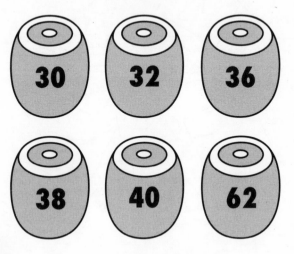

see answer
26

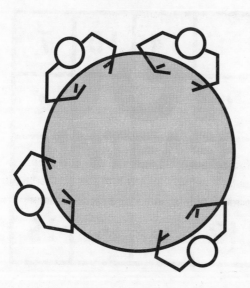

Four people are seated around a table. Where should you be seated in order to be the greatest overall distance from all four people measured around the edge of the table?

see answer
58

The numbers 4–16 have already been inserted into the grid, almost – but not quite – at random. Following just two simple rules, where would you place the numbers 1, 2 and 3 in the grid?

see answer
44

Study Time

Three college students — Anne, Bess and Candice — each study four subjects. Two of them study physics; two study algebra; two study English; two study history; two study French; two study Japanese.

Anne: if she studies algebra then she also takes history;
          if she studies history she does not take English;
          if she studies English she does not take Japanese.

Candice: if she studies French she does not take algebra;
          if she does not study algebra she studies Japanese;
          if she studies Japanese she does not take English.

Bess: if she studies English she also takes Japanese;
          if she studies Japanese she does not take algebra;
          if she studies algebra she does not take French.

What do you know about these three students?

	ANNE	BESS	CANDICE
PHYSICS			
ALGEBRA			
ENGLISH			
HISTORY			
FRENCH			
JAPANESE			

see answer
47

Mr Carter, Mr Butler, Mr Drover and Mr Hunter are employed as a carter, a butler, a drover and a hunter. None of them has a name identifying their profession, though. They made four statements:

1. Mr Carter is the hunter.
2. Mr Drover is the carter.
3. Mr Butler is not the hunter.
4. Mr Hunter is not the butler.

According to those statements, the butler must be Mr Butler, but this cannot be correct. Three of the four statements are untrue. Who is the drover?

see answer
49

Mr Peters, Mr Edwards and Mr Roberts are playing a round of golf together. Half-way through the game Mr Peters remarks that he has just noticed that their first names are Peter, Edward and Robert.

"Yes," says one of the others, "I'd noticed that too, but none of us has the same surname as our own first name. For example, my first name is Robert."

What are the full names of the three golfers?

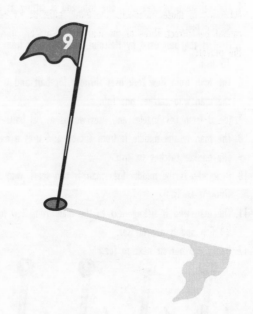

see answer
50

Five men staying at a coastal hotel decide to go fishing on the pier. They sit next to each other, using different bait, and catch different numbers of fish.

1. The plumber, called Henry, catches one fish fewer than Dick.
2. The electrician is next to the banker and uses bread for his bait.
3. The man at the north end of the pier is the banker, who is sitting next to Fred.
4. The salesman catches only one fish, and is sitting at the south end of the pier.
5. Meal is the bait used by Malcolm, and the man from Orlando catches 15 fish.
6. The man from New York uses shrimps for bait and is sitting next to the man who catches one fish.
7. Joe is from Los Angeles and uses worms as his bait.
8. The man in the middle is from Tucson and uses a bait of maggots.
9. The banker catches six fish.
10. Dick, who is the middle fisherman, is two seats away from the man from St Louis.
11. The man who is sitting next to the man from New York catches 10 fish and is a professor.
12. Henry did not sit next to Joe.

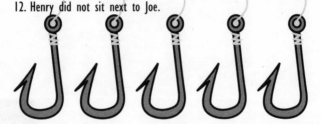

Gone Fishing

Work out where each man lives, his occupation, the bait he is using, and how many fish he catches.

NORTH ◄——————— PIER ———————► SOUTH

NAME				
OCCUPATION				
TOWN				
BAIT				
CATCH				

see answer
54

A man can drink a barrel of beer in 27 days.
A woman can drink a barrel of beer in 54 days.

If they both drink out of the same barrel at their respective rates, how long will it take for the barrel to be emptied?

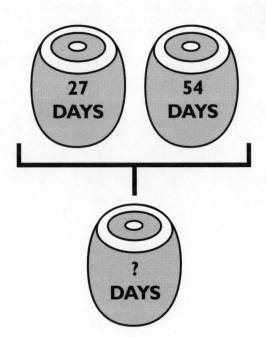

see answer
63

Bill says to Jim, "Let's have a wager on each frame. We will play for half of the money in your wallet on each frame, and we will have 10 frames. Since you have $8 in your wallet, we will play for $4 on the first frame. I will give you $4 if you win and you will give me $4 if I win. When we start the second frame you will have either $12 or $4, so we will play for $6 or $2, etc."

They play 10 frames. Bill wins four and loses six frames but Jim finds that he has only $5.70 left and so has lost $2.30. How is this possible?

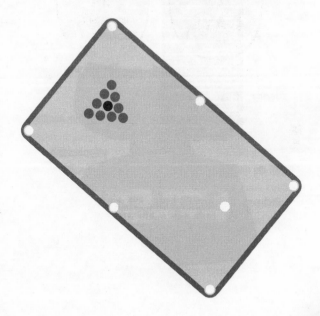

see answer
55

Pleased Pupils

There are five pupils, each in a different class. Each pupil takes a subject and sport which she enjoys.

		CLASS					SUBJECT					SPORT				
		2	3	4	5	6	HISTORY	ALGEBRA	CHEMISTRY	GEOGRAPHY	BIOLOGY	TENNIS	SQUASH	SWIMMING	RUNNING	BASKETBALL
NAME	ALICE															
	BETTY															
	CLARA															
	DORIS															
	ELIZABETH															
SPORT	TENNIS															
	SQUASH															
	SWIMMING															
	RUNNING															
	BASKETBALL															
SUBJECT	HISTORY															
	ALGEBRA															
	CHEMISTRY															
	GEOGRAPHY															
	BIOLOGY															

Pleased Pupils

1. The girl who plays squash likes algebra and is not in class 5.
2. Doris is in class 3 and Betty likes running.
3. The girl who likes running is in class 2.
4. The girl in class 4 likes swimming, and Elizabeth likes chemistry.
5. Alice is in class 6 and likes squash but not geography.
6. The girl who likes chemistry also enjoys basketball.
7. The girl who likes biology also likes running.
8. Clara likes history but not tennis.

Work out the class, subject and sport of each girl.

NAME	CLASS	SUBJECT	SPORT

see answer
52

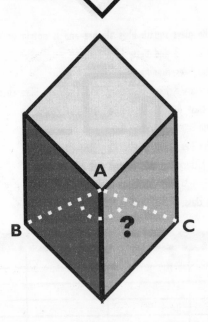

Two diagonals have been drawn on two faces of the cube. Using logical reasoning and lateral thinking, can you work out the angle between the two diagonals AB and AC?

see answer
62

A clock on the wall falls to the floor and the face breaks into three pieces. The digits on each piece of clock add up to the same total. What are the digits on each piece?

see answer
51

Changing Trains

A woman usually leaves work at 5.30pm, calls at the supermarket, then catches the 6pm train, which arrives at the station in her home town at 6.30pm. Her husband leaves home each day, drives to the station and picks her up at 6.30pm, just as she gets off the train.

Today the woman finishes work about five minutes earlier than usual, decides to go straight to the station instead of calling at the supermarket, and manages to catch the 5.30pm train, which arrives at her home station at 6pm. Since her husband is not there to pick her up she begins to walk home. Her husband leaves home at the usual time, sees his wife walking, turns around, picks her up and drives home, arriving there 10 minutes earlier than usual.

Assume that all the trains arrive precisely on time. For how long does the woman walk before her husband picks her up?

see answer
59

Each of the nine squares in the grid marked 1A to 3C should incorporate all the lines and symbols which are shown in the squares of the same letter and number immediately above and to the left. For example, 2B should incorporate all the lines and symbols that are in square 2 and square B.

One of the squares is incorrect. Which is it?

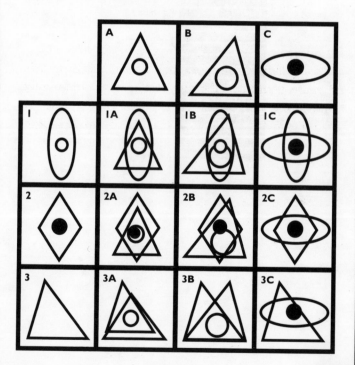

see answer
57

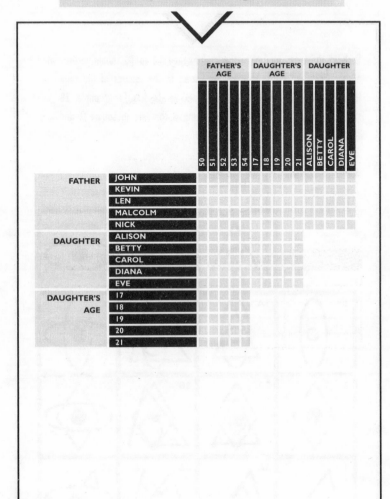

		FATHER'S AGE					DAUGHTER'S AGE					DAUGHTER				
		50	51	52	53	54	17	18	19	20	21	ALISON	BETTY	CAROL	DIANA	EVE
FATHER	JOHN															
	KEVIN															
	LEN															
	MALCOLM															
	NICK															
DAUGHTER	ALISON															
	BETTY															
	CAROL															
	DIANA															
	EVE															
DAUGHTER'S AGE	17															
	18															
	19															
	20															
	21															

A group of friends get together with their daughters for the evening.

1. John is 52 years old and his daughter is not called Eve.
2. Len has a daughter aged 21, and Betty is three years older than Eve.
3. Kevin is 53 years old and Diana is 19 years old.
4. Eve is 18 years old, and Nick has a daughter called Carol.
5. Alison is 20 years old and her father is called John.
6. Kevin has a daughter aged 19, and Eve's father is called Malcolm.
7. Malcolm is three years older than Nick.

FATHER	DAUGHTER	FATHER'S AGE	DAUGHTER'S AGE

see answer
60

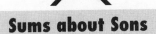
A woman has two sons, Graham and Frederick. Frederick is three times as old as Graham. If you square Frederick's age you arrive at the same total as when you cube Graham's age. If you subtract Graham's age from Frederick's you arrive at the number of steps in the path to the family's front door. If you add Graham's age to Frederick's you arrive at the number of palisades in the family's fence. If you multiply their ages you arrive at the number of bricks in the family's front wall.

If you add these last three numbers together you have the family's house number, which is 297.

How old are Graham and Frederick?

see answer
61

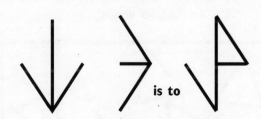

is to

as

is to:

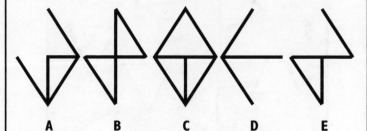

A   B   C   D   E

see answer
43

What is the smallest number of segments of equal area and shape that the rectangle can be divided into so that each segment contains the same number of triangles?

see answer
48

Which of these circles is the odd one out?

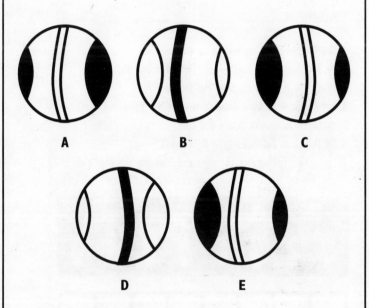

A   B   C

D   E

see answer
46

Four husband and wife couples go to see a play. They all sit in the same row, but no husband sits next to his wife, and a man and a woman are at opposite ends of the row. Their surnames are Andrews, Barker, Collins and Dunlop.

1. Mrs Dunlop or Mr Andrews is in the end seat.
2. Mr Andrews is mid-way between Mr Collins and Mrs Collins.
3. Mr Collins is two seats from Mrs Dunlop.
4. Mrs Collins is mid-way between Mr and Mrs Barker.
5. Mrs Andrews is next to the end seat.
6. Mr Dunlop is two seats from Mr Andrews.
7. Mrs Collins is closer to the right end than the left end.

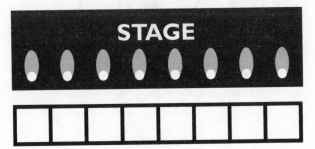

Work out the seating arrangements along the row.

Feed information into the seats clue by clue.

1							
2							
3							
4							
5							
6							
7							

see answer
45

Five sailors of different rank are at different ports on different ships.

		RANK					SHIP					LOCATION				
		COMMANDER	CAPTAIN	STEWARD	PURSER	SEAMAN	CRUISER	WARSHIP	FRIGATE	SUBMARINE	AIRCRAFT CARRIER	MALTA	CRETE	FALKLANDS	GIBRALTAR	PORTSMOUTH
NAME	PERKINS															
	WARD															
	MANNING															
	DEWHURST															
	BRAND															
LOCATION	MALTA															
	CRETE															
	FALKLANDS															
	GIBRALTAR															
	PORTSMOUTH															
SHIP	CRUISER															
	WARSHIP															
	FRIGATE															
	SUBMARINE															
	AIRCRAFT CARRIER															

Hello, Sailor

1. Manning is at the Falklands, and the purser is Dewhurst.
2. Brand is on a warship, and the purser is not on the cruiser.
3. Perkins is on the aircraft carrier, and Ward is at Portsmouth.
4. The commander is at the Falklands, and Manning is on a submarine.
5. The warship is at Crete, and Perkins is at Malta.
6. The frigate is at Gibraltar and the steward is at Malta.
7. Brand is a captain and the seaman is not on the frigate.

Work out the details of each sailor.

NAME	RANK	SHIP	LOCATION

see answer
53

Which of the following shapes is the odd one out?

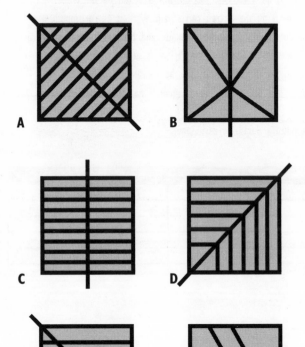

A   B

C   D

E   F

see answer
56

A   B

In Broadway, New York City, a man saw a new type of bus, as shown above. It was stationary and he could not tell which way it was going.

Can you?

see answer
74

The clocks above follow a weird kind of logic. What time should the fourth clock show? Choose from the four options provided.

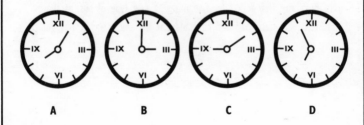

see answer
73

Round and Round the Garden

A woman has a garden path 2m wide, with a hedge on either side. The path spirals into the middle of the garden. One day the woman walks the length of the path, finishing in the middle. Ignore the width of the hedge and assume she walks in the middle of the path. How far does she walk?

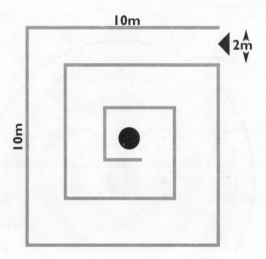

10m

2m

10m

see answer
80

Three soldiers — Colonel Ketchup, Major Mustard and Captain Chutney — have a shooting competition. They each fire six shots, shown below, and each score 71 points. Colonel Ketchup's first two shots score 22; Major Mustard's first shot scores 3.

Who hits the bull's eye?

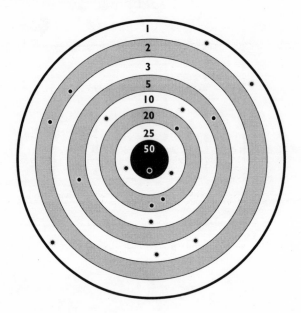

see answer
67

74882	3584	

29637		192

74826		

Fill in the missing numbers from the bars above. Just enough information has been provided to work out the logic. The logic is the same in each line of numbers.

Now try this one:

528	116	

793		335

821		

see answer
76

81

Bully Bill and Dynamo Dan are cattle ranchers. One day they decide to sell their stock and become sheep farmers. They take the cattle to market and receive for each steer a number of dollars equal to the total number of steer that they sell. With this money they purchase sheep at $10 per head, and with the money left over they purchase a goat.

On the way home they argue and so decide to divide up their stock, but find that they have one sheep over. So Bully Bill keeps the sheep and gives Dynamo Dan the goat.

"But I have less than you," says Dynamo Dan, "because a goat is worth less than a sheep."

"Alright," says Bully Bill, "I will give you my Colt .45 to make up the difference."

What is the value of the Colt .45?

see answer
65

Black and White Balls

This probability problem can be solved through logical thought.

You have two bags, each one containing eight balls: four white and four black. A ball is drawn out of bag one and another ball out of bag two.

What are the chances that at least one of the balls is black?

BAG ONE

BAG TWO

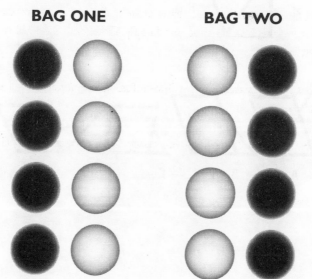

see answer
70

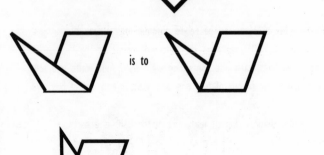

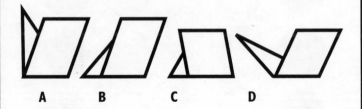

A   B   C   D

see answer
83

Dice Dilemma

Here are views of six non-standard, six-sided dice. Which of the dice can not be made up from the flattened version at the bottom?

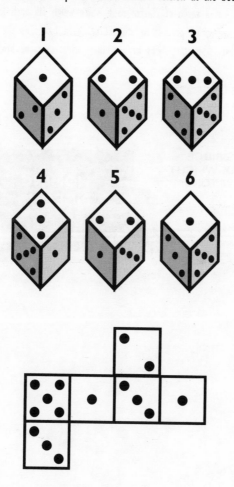

see answer 82

Carrier Pigeons

As a driver approaches a bridge, he notices that the maximum weight allowed is 20 tons. He knows that his empty truck weighs 20 tons. However, he has a cargo of 200 pigeons, which weigh 1lb each. As the pigeons are asleep on perches he stops the vehicle, bangs on the side to wake the birds, who start flying around, then drives over the bridge.

Is he correct?

BRIDGE
MAX. WEIGHT
20 TONS

HOMING
PIGEONS

see answer
71

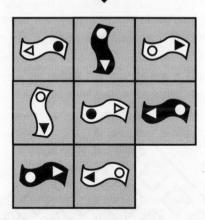

Look along each line and down each column above and work out which is the missing square from these options:

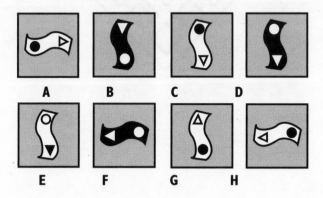

A B C D

E F G H

see answer
64

City blocks have been built between two main roads — A and B — in a grid, like Manhattan, New York. Always moving toward B, how many different routes are there?

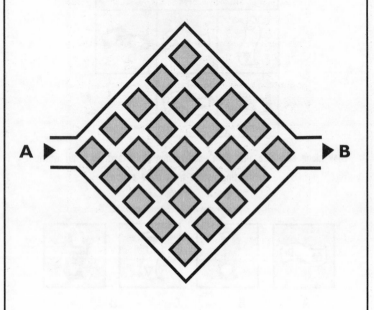

see answer
77

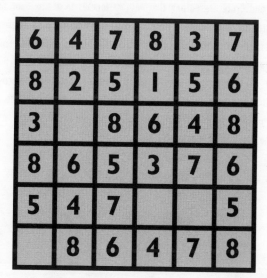

There is a logic behind the distribution of numbers in the grid. Work out what it is and then fill in the missing numbers.

see answer
66

Patrick and Bruce are putting the finishing touches to a new door they have fitted to house number 4761. All that is left to do is to screw the four metal digits to the door. Being a Mensan, Patrick could not resist challenging Bruce by asking him if he could screw the digits onto the door to give a four-figure number which could not be divided exactly by 9. When they had resolved that puzzle, Bruce then asked Patrick if he could screw the same digits onto the door to give a four-figure number which could not be divided exactly by 3.

What are the answers to the two puzzles? Can either of them be done?

see answer
81

Star Gazing

What is the largest star that can be drawn so that it is in the same proportions as the other stars and does not touch another star or overlap the edges of the border?

see answer
78

Skyscraper Sizzler

A woman lives in a skyscraper 36 floors high and served by several elevators, which stop at each floor going up and down. Each morning she leaves her apartment on one of the floors and goes to one of the elevators. Whichever one she takes is three times more likely to be going up than down.

Why is this?

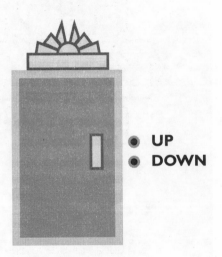

UP
DOWN

see answer
69

Round the Hexagons

Can you work out what should be the contents of the top hexagon?

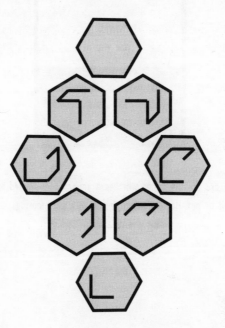

Choose from these options.

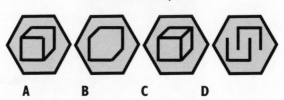

A   B   C   D

68

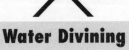

Two men are arguing about whether a square open-topped water tank is half full or not. How can they decide without removing the water or using any measuring device?

see answer
75

Bartender's Beer

A man goes into a bar in New York.

"Glass of beer, please," he says to the bartender.

"Light or special?" asks the bartender.

"What's the difference?" asks the man.

"Light is 90 cents, special is $1," replies the bartender.

"I'll have the special," says the man, placing $1 on the counter.

Another man comes into the bar.

"Glass of beer, please," he says, placing $1 on the counter.

The bartender gives him the special.

Why would he do that?

see answer
72

Pyramid Puzzle

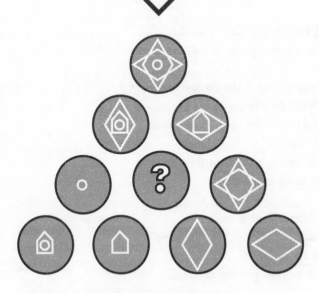

Look at the sequence of shapes above.
Which of the following options carries on the sequence?

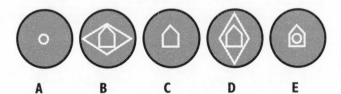

A   B   C   D   E

see answer
79

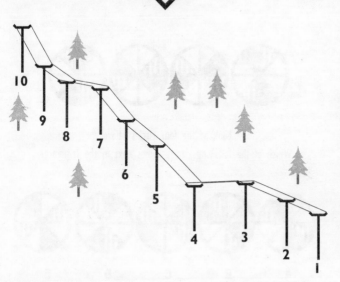

There are 10 places to embark and disembark on the ski-lift at this ski resort. It is possible to purchase a single ticket between any two stations.

How many different tickets are needed for skiers to go to every station from every other station?

see answer
84

Look at the four circles above.
Which of the following circles comes next in the sequence?

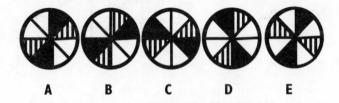

A   B   C   D   E

see answer
110

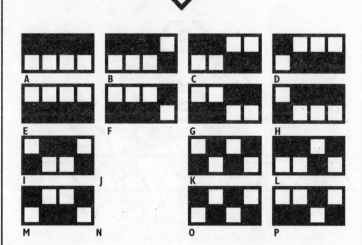

A   B   C   D
E   F   G   H
I   J   K   L
M   N   O   P

Look at the above sequence.
Which of options 1–6 becomes J and which N?

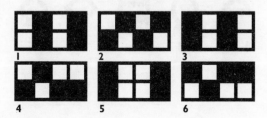

1   2   3
4   5   6

see answer
86

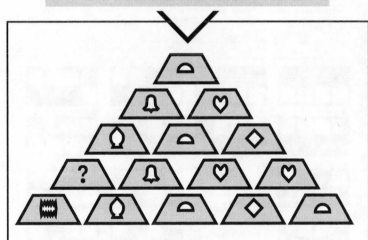

Look at the pyramid above.
Which of the following symbols should replace the question mark?

A   B   C   D   E

see answer
89

Pentagon Figures

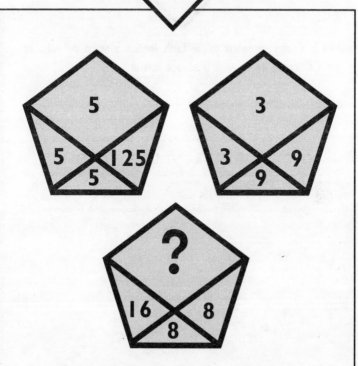

What number should replace the question mark above?

see answer
101

There is a valley somewhere on the Earth. The Sun is nearer the valley by over 4,800km at noon than it is when it rises or sets.

Where is this valley?

see answer
91

Lonely Loser

Which of the following figures is the odd one out?

A

B

C

D

E

see answer
96

At the fairground there is a competition — you purchase a ticket on which there is a number of scratch-off squares. One square is marked "loser"; two others have identical symbols. If these appear before the loser square appears, you win a prize. The odds against winning are 2:1 against.

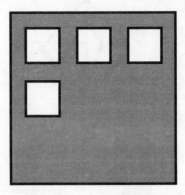

How many squares are on the card?

see answer
97

What number should replace the question mark in the last circle?

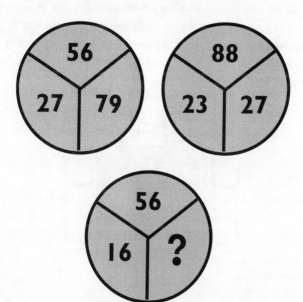

see answer
94

Dinner Party Placements

Mr and Mrs Ackrington, Mr and Mrs Blackpool, Mr and Mrs Chester and Mr and Mrs Doncaster are attending a dinner party. Only one couple does not sit next to each other, and this couple does not sit across from each other. The person sitting opposite Mrs Accrington is a man who is sitting immediately to the left of Mr Blackpool. The person sitting on Mrs Chester's immediate left is a man who is sitting across from Mr Doncaster.

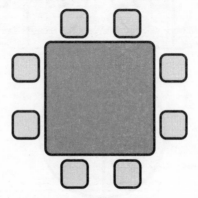

Which couple does not sit next to each other?

see answer
87

Square Sort

This grid consists of three squares marked A, B and C, and three squares marked 1, 2 and 3. The nine inner squares should incorporate the lines and symbols of both the letter and the number squares. One of the nine squares is incorrect. Which is it?

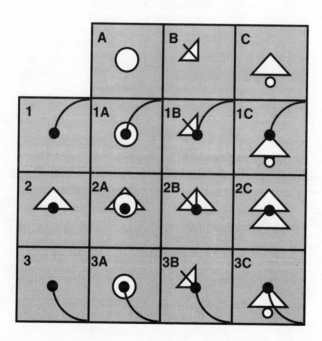

see answer
109

I am four times as old as my daughter.
In 20 years time I shall be twice as old as her.
How old are we now?

see answer
93

Five Circles

All five circles above have the same diameter. Draw a line moving through point A in such a way that it divides the five circles into two groups with equal areas.

see answer
105

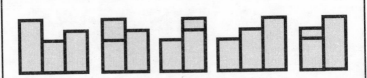

Look at the shapes above.
Does option A, B, C, D or E continue the sequence?

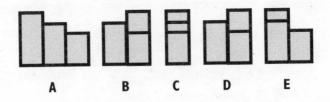

A   B   C   D   E

see answer
99

Look at the three squares above.
Does option A, B, C, D, E or F continue the sequence?

A

B

C

D

E

F

see answer
92

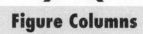

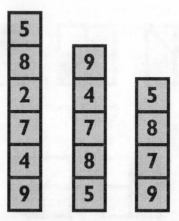

| 5 |
| 8 |
| 2 |
| 7 |
| 4 |
| 9 |

| 9 |
| 4 |
| 7 |
| 8 |
| 5 |

| 5 |
| 8 |
| 7 |
| 9 |

Look at the three columns of figures above.
Which column comes next in the sequence?

| 7 |
| 8 |
| 5 |

| 8 |
| 7 |
| 9 |

| 9 |
| 8 |
| 5 |

| 9 |
| 7 |
| 8 |

A   B   C   D

see answer
90

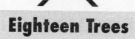

Eighteen Trees

A gardener has 18 trees which he wishes to plant in a variety of straight rows of five trees per row. He sets himself the task of planting the 18 trees in such an arrangement that he will obtain the maximum number of rows of five trees per row.

There are two slightly different ways he can do this.
Can you find both ways?

see answer
103

Replace the question mark with the missing number.

see answer
100

Counting Creatures

At the zoo there are penguins and huskies next to each other.
In all, I can count 72 creatures and 200 legs.

How many penguins are there?

see answer
102

is to

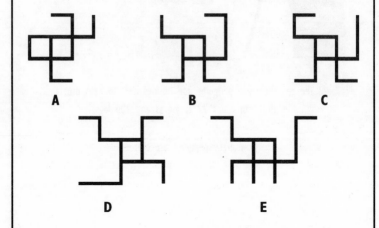

A   B   C

D   E

see answer
106

Chess Strategy

A master has to win two games of chess in a row in order to win a prize. In total, he has to play only three games, alternating between a strong opponent, who he can sometimes beat, and a weak opponent, who he can always beat. Should he play strong, weak, strong; or weak, strong, weak?

see answer
95

Careful Calculation

If the upper pair of numbers total 9825, what do the lower pair of numbers total?

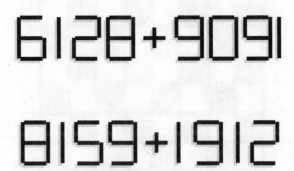

6128+9091

8159+1912

see answer
88

Number Crunching

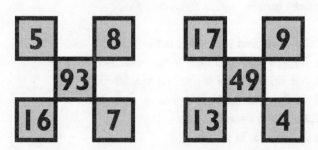

Look at these diagrams. What number should replace the question mark below?

see answer
108

Five pilots take their flights from five different UK airports to five different countries.

1. The aircraft from Stansted flies to Nice.
2. The flight from Cardiff has a captain named Paul.
3. Mike flies to JFK, New York, but not from Gatwick.
4. The flight from Manchester does not go to the USA.
5. Nick flies to Vancouver.
6. Paul does not fly to Roma.
7. Nick does not fly from Manchester.
8. Robin does not fly from Stansted.
9. The flight from Heathrow, not piloted by Tony, is not for Berlin.

Can you sort them out?

Five Pilots

NAME	AIRPORT	DESTINATION

see answer 85

Frogs and Flies

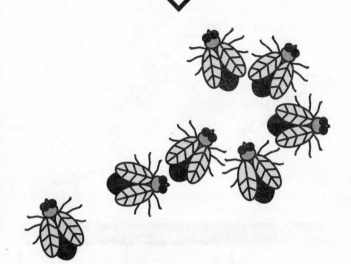

If 29 frogs catch 29 flies in 29 minutes, how many frogs are required to catch 87 flies in 87 minutes?

see answer
98

Island Access

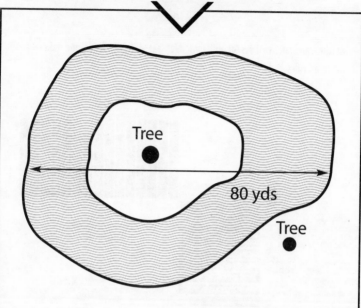

80 yds

There is a lake with an island in the middle.
On the island is a tree. The lake is deep and is 80 yards in
diameter. There is another tree on the mainland. A non-swimmer wishes to
get across to the island, but all he has is a length of rope 300 yards long.

How does he get across?

Fairground Fiesta

At the carnival five boys of different ages eat different foods and take different rides.

		AGE					RIDE					FOOD				
		11	12	13	14	15	BIG DIPPER	DODGEMS	MOUNTAIN	WHIRLIGIG	CROCODILE	ICE CREAM	HOT DOG	CANDY FLOSS	FRIES	GUM
NAME	SAM															
	JOE															
	DON															
	LEN															
	RON															
FOOD	ICE CREAM															
	HOT DOG															
	CANDY FLOSS															
	FRIES															
	GUM															
RIDE	BIG DIPPER															
	DODGEMS															
	MOUNTAIN															
	WHIRLIGIG															
	CROCODILE															

Fairground Fiesta

1. Ron eats ice cream; Joe does not chew gum.
2. Sam, who is 14 years old, is not on the mountain.
3. The boy on the crocodile is 15 years old.
4. Len is not on the dodgems; Don is on the whirligig.
5. The boy eating ice cream is 13 years old.
6. The boy on the dodgems is eating a hot dog.
7. Joe eats fries on the big dipper.
8. Don, who is 12, is eating candy floss.

Work out the details of each boy.

NAME	AGE	RIDE	FOOD

see answer
104

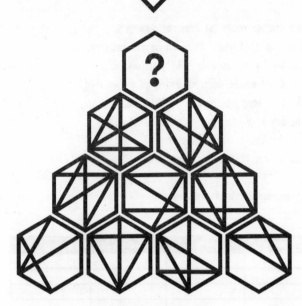

Look at the pyramid above.
From the following options, choose the contents of the top hexagon.

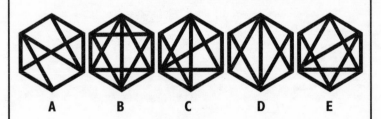

A   B   C   D   E

see answer
116

Look at the four circles above.
Should A, B, C, D or E continue the sequence?

A   B

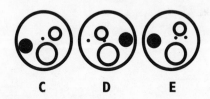

C   D   E

see answer
111

127

Strange Series

What is the next figure in this series?

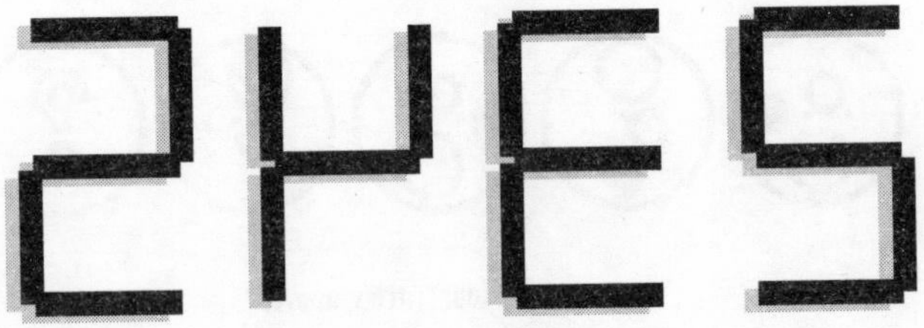

see answer
124

Which of these shapes is the odd one out?

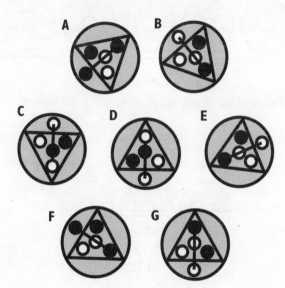

see answer
113

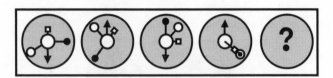

Look at the first four circles above.
Which of the following options comes next in the sequence?

A   **B**   **C**

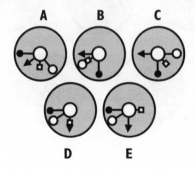

D   **E**

see answer
117

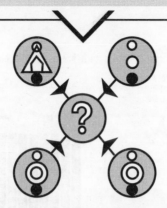

Each line and symbol which appears in the four outer circles is transferred to the middle circle according to a few rules. If a line or symbol occurs in the outer circles:

once, it is transferred;

twice, it is possibly transferred;

three times, it is transferred;

four times, it is not transferred.

Which of the following circles should appear at the centre of the diagram?

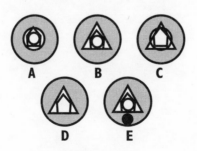

see answer
129

Bird Fanciers

Five men from different countries each like a different bird. Each bird has a different collective noun.

		COUNTRY					BIRD					COLLECTIVE NOUN				
		GERMANY	BELGIUM	FRANCE	ENGLAND	SCOTLAND	OWLS	PLOVERS	STARLINGS	CROWS	RAVENS	MURMURATION	WING	UNKINDNESS	MURDER	PARLIAMENT
NAME	ALBERT															
	ROGER															
	HAROLD															
	CAMERON															
	EDWARD															
COLLECTIVE NOUN	MURMURATION															
	WING															
	UNKINDNESS															
	MURDER															
	PARLIAMENT															
BIRD	OWLS															
	PLOVERS															
	STARLINGS															
	CROWS															
	RAVENS															

Bird Fanciers

1. Roger does not like plovers, which are not called a parliament.

2. The man who likes crows comes from France. This is not Edward, who is not from Scotland.

3. Albert likes owls; a group of starlings is called a murmuration.

4. Harold comes from Germany and likes ravens.

5. The man from England likes starlings.

6. Edward does not like the group called an unkindness of ravens.

7. The man who likes the group called murder comes from France.

8. Cameron is not from Belgium; Albert is not from Scotland.

9. The man who likes the group called wing is not from Germany.

Work out the details for each man.

NAME	COUNTRY	BIRDS	COLLECTIVE NOUN

see answer
114

Correct this equation so that it makes sense by freely moving the given four digits but without introducing any additional mathematical symbols.

$$76 = 24$$

see answer
112

Consider the three trominoes above.
Now choose one of the following to accompany them.

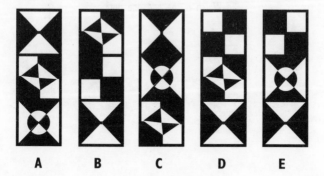

A   B   C   D   E

see answer
119

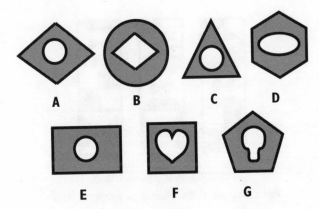

Which is the odd one out?

see answer
127

What is the missing number?

see answer
121

Following Fun

Look at the sequence below.
Which of the labelled options comes next?

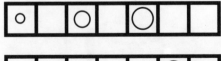

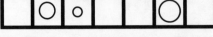

A

B

C

D

E

see answer
128

Triangle Teaser

Work out the three missing numbers in the third triangle.

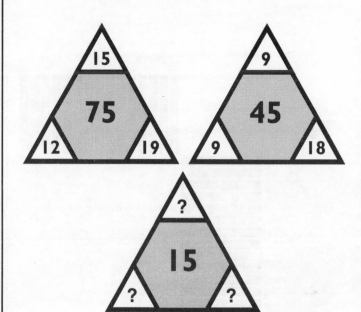

see answer
122

Household Items

Five women each purchase a household item for use in a different room in their house.

		SURNAME					ITEM					ROOM				
		WILLIAMS	SIMPSON	PRINGLE	DINGLE	GRIGGS	TELEVISION	BOOKCASE	HI-FI	COMPUTER	TELEPHONE	LIVING ROOM	KITCHEN	CONSERVATORY	BEDROOM	STUDY
FIRST NAME	KYLIE															
	AMY															
	CLARA															
	MICHELLE															
	ROXANNE															
ROOM	LIVING ROOM															
	KITCHEN															
	CONSERVATORY															
	BEDROOM															
	STUDY															
ITEM	TELEVISION															
	BOOKCASE															
	HI-FI															
	COMPUTER															
	TELEPHONE															

1. Mrs Simpson does not keep her item in the bedroom.
2. Amy has a television; Mrs Griggs has a hi-fi.
3. Kylie does not keep her item in the bedroom.
4. Clara does not have a telephone.
5. Mrs Williams does not keep her item in the kitchen.
6. Kylie keeps hers in the conservatory.
7. Michelle has a bookcase; Mrs Dingle has a computer.
8. Michelle does not keep hers in the living room.
9. Mrs Pringle keeps hers in the study; Roxanne keeps hers in the kitchen.

Can you work out the full name of each woman, her item and where she keeps it?

FIRST NAME	SURNAME	ROOM	ITEM

see answer
118

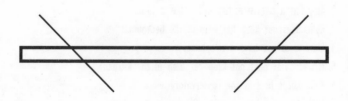

A stick breaks into three pieces. Without measuring the pieces or trying to construct a triangle, how can you quickly determine whether the pieces will form a triangle?

see answer

125

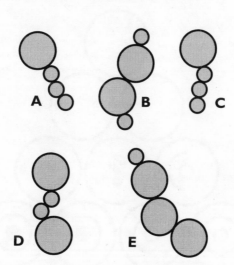

Which is the odd one out?

see answer
130

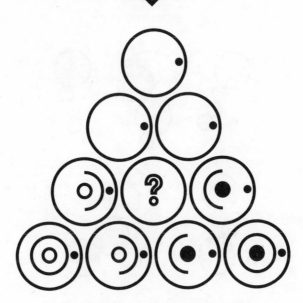

Consider the pyramid above.
Which of the following five options replaces the question mark?

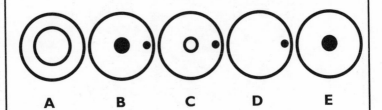

A   B   C   D   E

see answer
120

Perpetuate the Pattern

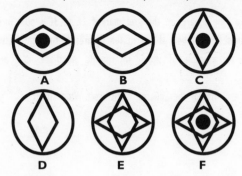

Which circle from the options below fits into the
blank space above to carry on the pattern?

see answer
115

Gritty Grid

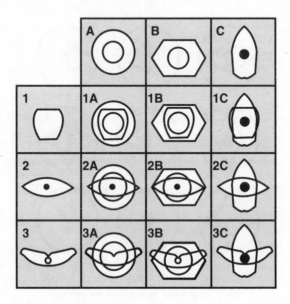

Each of the nine squares in the grid marked 1A to 3C should incorporate all the lines and symbols shown in the squares of the same letter and number. For example, 3C should incorporate the shapes in 3 and C.

One of the squares is incorrect. Which is it?

see answer
123

Fancy Figures

Find a logical reason for arranging these numbers into four groups of three numbers each:

**106 168 181 217 218 251 349
375 433 457 532 713**

GROUP 1	GROUP 2	GROUP 3	GROUP 4

see answer
126

Changing Shape

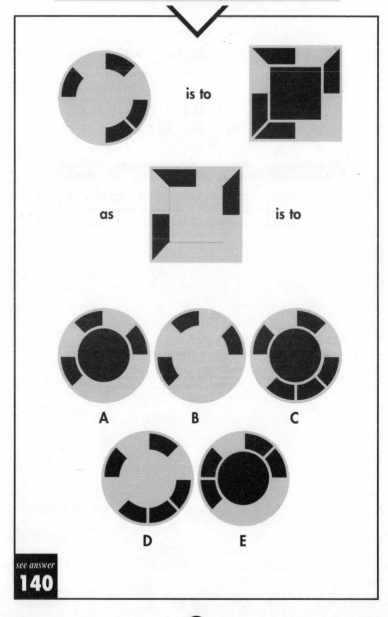

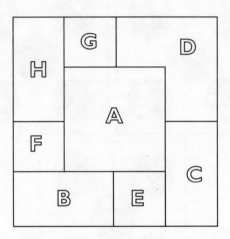

Eight square pieces of paper, all exactly the same size, have been placed on top of one another in a particular order so that they overlap as shown. List the order in which they have been positioned, working from the top sheet down to the bottom sheet.

see answer
133

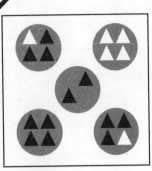

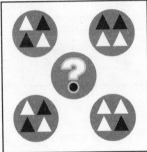

In the figure above, which of the following circles replaces the question mark?

A   B   C   D   E

see answer
135

Two-tone Teaser

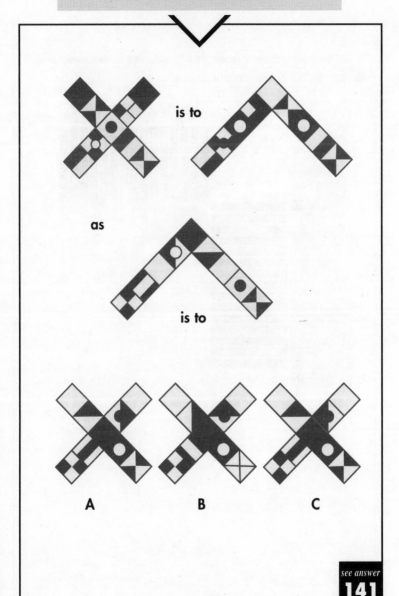

is to

as

is to

A   B   C

see answer
141

151

Creature Comforts

In the North live different creatures, each of which has its own particular characteristic and its own particular treasure.

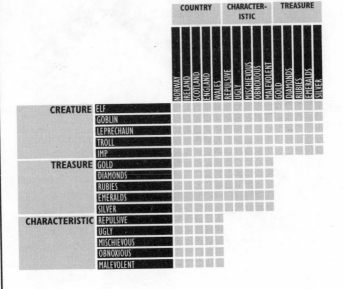

Creature Comforts

1. Leprechauns are mischievous; rubies come from Scotland.
2. Imps have silver; elves come from Norway.
3. Scotland has trolls; goblins have gold.
4. Elves are malevolent; Scotland has obnoxious creatures.
5. Goblins are repulsive; imps come from England.
6. Goblins are not ugly; Wales has no mischievous creatures.
7. Ireland has no diamonds.

Work out each creature's, characteristic, its treasure and the country it lives in.

CREATURE	COUNTRY	CHARACTERISTIC	TREASURE

see answer
146

To which of the five boxes below can a dot be added so that both dots then meet the same conditions as the box above?

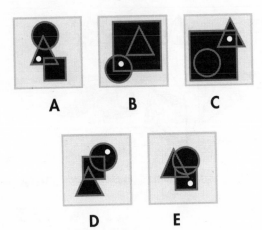

A   B   C

D   E

Stocking Search

A woman has 43 stockings in her drawer: 21 blue, 8 black and 14 striped. She has fused the lights and cannot see into the drawer.

How many stockings must she take out to make certain that she has a pair of each?

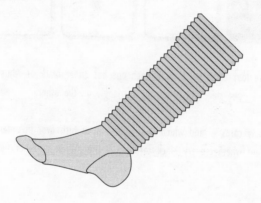

see answer
147

1   **2**   **3**   **4**

There are four cards on a table. Each one has either black or white on one side, and a star or a triangle on the other.

How many cards — and which ones — must you turn over in order to work out whether every black card has a triangle on its other side?

see answer
143

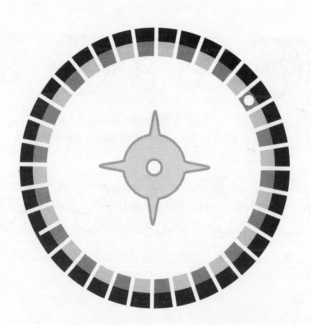

A casino uses only $5 and $8 chips on its standard roulette wheel.

What is the largest wager that cannot be placed?

see answer
144

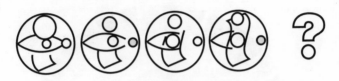

Look at the circles above.
Which of the following options comes next in the sequence?

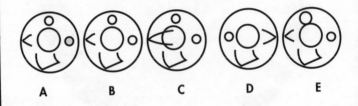

A   B   C   D   E

see answer
145

Diamond Division

Divide the diamond into four equal shapes, each containing one of each of the following five symbols:

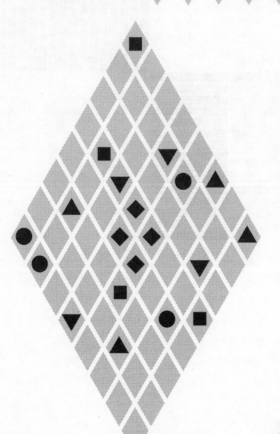

see answer
149

Fabulous Football

Five players each play for a different team in a different position, and each wears a different shirt.

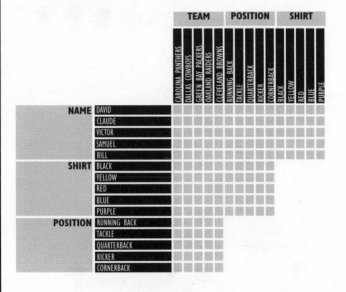

		TEAM					POSITION					SHIRT				
		CAROLINA PANTHERS	DALLAS COWBOYS	GREEN BAY PACKERS	OAKLAND RAIDERS	CLEVELAND BROWNS	RUNNING BACK	TACKLE	QUARTERBACK	KICKER	CORNERBACK	BLACK	YELLOW	RED	BLUE	PURPLE
NAME	DAVID															
	CLAUDE															
	VICTOR															
	SAMUEL															
	BILL															
SHIRT	BLACK															
	YELLOW															
	RED															
	BLUE															
	PURPLE															
POSITION	RUNNING BACK															
	TACKLE															
	QUARTERBACK															
	KICKER															
	CORNERBACK															

1. The Carolina Panthers player wears a purple shirt.
2. Samuel is not a running back; the tackle plays for the Dallas Cowboys.
3. The quarterback wears yellow; Claude plays for the Dallas Cowboys.
4. The kicker does not play for the Green Bay Packers.
5. David does not play for the Oakland Raiders; Samuel wears black.
6. The cornerback is at the Oakland Raiders; David plays in yellow.
7. Victor is in the Cleveland Browns and does not wear blue.
8. Bill is the kicker, and the Cleveland Browns player wears red.

Can you work out the details?

NAME	TEAM	POSITION	SHIRT

see answer
148

From the clues below, work out each woman's full name, the name of her house and the shade of its front door.

1. Mrs Rivers' name is not Tracy, and her front door is not red.
2. Mrs Manby's name is Cheryl and she does not live at The White House.
3. Chez Nous does not have a black door, and neither does Mrs Hill's house.
4. Peggy's house has a green door and is not Rose Cottage.
5. Cheryl's house does not have a red door, but Hill House does.
6. Mabel's house has a blue door, but her name is not Mrs Sullivan.
7. Tracy's house is named Riverside.
8. Mrs Stevens' house is called Rose Cottage.
9. Grace's front door is not orange.
10. Dorothy does not live at Valley View, which does not have a green door.
11. Mrs Sullivan lives at Valley View and does not have a black door.
12. Mrs Peters does not have a white door.

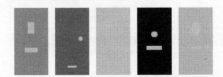

FIRST NAME	SURNAME	HOUSE NAME	FRONT DOOR

see answer
139

Five murder suspects, including the guilty party, are being interrogated by the police at the scene of a brutal murder. Of the five statements made, just three are the truth.

Who committed the murder?

ALF WHITE	"David Dark is the murderer."
BARRY GLOOMY	"I am innocent."
CYRIL SHADY	"It wasn't Ernie Black."
DAVID DARK	"Alf White is lying."
ERNIE BLACK	"Barry Gloomy is telling the truth."

see answer
137

Coveted Cars

Five friends have cars made in different years, of different paint finishes and different upholstery.

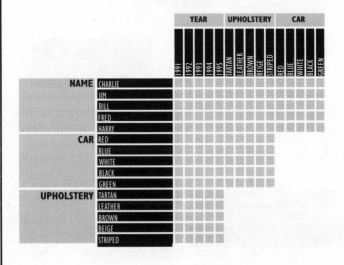

		YEAR					UPHOLSTERY					CAR				
		1991	1992	1993	1994	1995	TARTAN	LEATHER	BROWN	BEIGE	STRIPED	RED	BLUE	WHITE	BLACK	GREEN
NAME	CHARLIE															
	JIM															
	BILL															
	FRED															
	HARRY															
CAR	RED															
	BLUE															
	WHITE															
	BLACK															
	GREEN															
UPHOLSTERY	TARTAN															
	LEATHER															
	BROWN															
	BEIGE															
	STRIPED															

1. The car made in 1993 has tartan upholstery.
2. The car with brown upholstery is blue.
3. Harry's car is red, with striped upholstery, and was made in 1991.
4. Fred's car is older than Charlie's car, which is green.
5. Jim's car was made in 1992.
6. The car with leather upholstery is white and does not belong to Bill.
7. Bill's car, which was built in 1994, is not black.

For each person, work out the year their car was made, its paint finish and style of upholstery.

NAME	YEAR	UPHOLSTERY	CAR

see answer
138

Drawing Dominoes

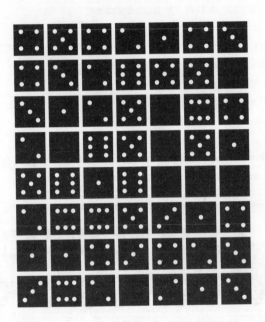

Draw lines in this box to reveal 28 dominoes, as follows:

0–0						
0–1	1–1					
0–2	1–2	2–2				
0–3	1–3	2–3	3–3			
0–4	1–4	2–4	3–4	4–4		
0–5	1–5	2–5	3–5	4–5	5–5	
0–6	1–6	2–6	3–6	4–6	5–6	6–6

see answer
134

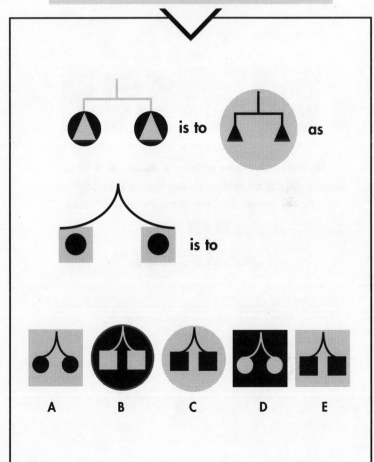

see answer
150

The tiler at the ceramics exhibition is showing sets of cut tiles.
Somebody requests his telephone number, which is a seven-digit number.
The tiler arranges some tiles so that the telephone number
may easily be read.

What is his telephone number?

see answer
131

Sweet Sequence

Look at the three drawings above.
Which of options A, B, C or D continues the sequence?

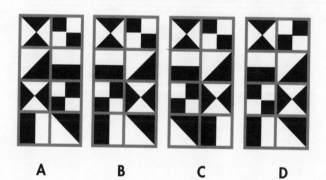

A   B   C   D

see answer
136

Probability Paradox

This puzzle requires no prior knowledge about the rules of probability and can be solved by logical reasoning.

Four balls are placed in a bag. One is black, one white and the other two red. The bag is shaken and someone draws two balls from the bag. He looks at the two balls and announces that one of them is red.

What are the chances that the other ball he has drawn out is also red?

see answer
132

Answer 1
Las Vegas
Each gambler's die was numbered as follows:
Diablo: 6 – 1 – 8 – 6 – 1 – 8
Scarface: 7 – 5 – 3 – 7 – 5 – 3
Lucky: 2 – 9 – 4 – 2 – 9 – 4
In a long run:
Diablo would win against Scarface 10 times in 18;
Scarface would win against Lucky 10 times in 18;
Lucky would win against Diablo 10 times in 18.

**Diablo v Scarface: 6–7; 1–7; 8–7 win; 6–5 win; 1–5; 8–5 win;
6–3 win; 1–3; 8–3 win, which, when repeated, gives 10 wins and 8
losses for Diablo.**
**Scarface v Lucky: 7–2 win; 5–2 win; 3–2 win; 7–9; 5–9; 3–9;
7–4 win; 5–4 win; 3–4, which, when repeated, gives 10 wins and 8
losses for Scarface.**
**Lucky v Diablo: 2–6; 9–6 win; 4–6; 2–1 win; 9–1 win; 4–1 win;
2–8; 9–8 win; 4–8, which, when repeated, gives 10 wins and 8 losses
to Lucky.**

Answer 2
Three Circles

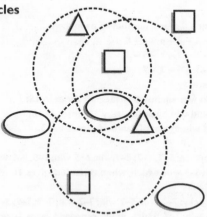

Answer 3
Town Clock

I forgot to mention that my clock was digital. One line was not functioning on the eight lines that make up each digit.

◀ THIS LINE NOT FUNCTIONING

	TIME SHOWED	SHOULD HAVE SHOWN
8.55	5	5
8.56	6	6
8.58	6 ◀ MISSING	8
8.59	5 ◀ MISSING	9
9.00	◀ MISSING	0

Answer 4
Booth Bonanza

If number eight did not require repairing the supervisor would have said that five out of the first seven needed repairing.

Answer 5
Tricky Triangles

E. There are four triangles constantly moving clockwise around the arms and visiting points in sequence.

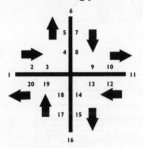

Answer 6
Murder in Mind

Alf Muggins. If it was Jack Vicious, the statements of Alf Muggins and Jim Pouncer would be true. If it was Sid Shifty, the statements of Jack Vicious, Alf Muggins and Jim Pouncer would be true. If it was Jim Pouncer, the statements of Sid Shifty and Alf Muggins would be true. Therefore it is Alf Muggins, and only the statement of Jim Pouncer is true.

Answer 7
Fancy Figures

2, 5, 7, 10, 12, 15, 17.

Answer 8
Hexagon Harmony

A. There are six triangles, each with their base on one of the sides of the hexagon. Each triangle increases in height by a quarter of the width of the hexagon at each stage. So, showing one triangle only:

Answer 9
Manor House

Name	Occupation	Pastime	Rest day
Smith	Butler	Squash	Friday
Jones	Gardener	Golf	Tuesday
Wood	Chauffeur	Fishing	Wednesday
Clark	Janitor	Chess	Thursday
James	Cook	Bridge	Monday

Answer 10
Converging Circles
C.

Answer 11
Sears Tower
450m.

Answer 12
Land of Zoz

What they say they are	Numbers in the group	What they actually are	What they become
Fibkins	30	30 Switchkins	30 Fibkins
Switchkins	15:15	15 Fibkins 15 Switchkins	15 Fibkins 15 Switchkins
Truthkins	10:10:10	10 Truthkins 10 Fibkins 10 Switchkins	10 Truthkins 10 Fibkins 10 Truthkins

55 Fibkins live in pentagonal houses that night.

Only Switchkins can claim to be Fibkins, as it would be a lie to a Truthkin, and the truth to a Fibkin. So the group which claimed to be Fibkins must be all Switchkins, and so must be the group of 30 x 1. The Switchkins of that group thus become Fibkins, because that's what they said they were. Similarly, only Fibkins or Switchkins can claim to be Switchkins, so the group that claimed to be Switchkins must be 15 Fibkins and 15 Switchkins, and the Switchkins stay as they are. That means that the group that claimed to be Truthkins is made up of all three types – all can claim to be Truthkins. The 10 Switchkins of this group become Truthkins. Therefore, at the end of the day there are 15 Switchkins (the 15 who told the truth about what they were), 20 Truthkins (10 original Truthkins, and 10 former Switchkins), and 55 Fibkins (10 who lied about being Truthkins, 15 who lied about being Switchkins, and the 30 former Switchkins who became Fibkins by claiming that was what they were). Pentagonal houses are used by Fibkins.

Answer 13
Making Eyes

D. There is a sequence occurring from the right eye to the left eye (as we look at them). Look at stages one and two. The contents of the eyes in stage one have merged to form the left eye of stage two and a new symbol has been introduced in the right eye of stage two. Now look at stages two and three. The contents of the left eye in stage two has moved away and does not appear in stage three. The symbol from the right eye in stage two has moved to fill the left eye of stage three and a new symbol has been introduced in the right eye of stage three. This pattern of change is then continued, so that the left eye of stage four contains a merging of both eyes in stage three.

Answer 14
Shooting Range

Colonel Present scored 200 (60, 60, 40, 40)
Major Aim scored 240 (60, 60, 60, 60)
General Fire scored 180 (60, 40, 40, 40)

The incorrect statements made by each marksman are as follows:
Colonel Present, statement number 1;
Major Aim, statement number 3;
General Fire, statement number 3.

Answer 15
Counterfeit Coins

Only one weighing operation is necessary. You take one coin from bag one, two coins from bag two and three coins from bag three and weigh all six coins together. If they weigh 305g the first bag contains the counterfeit coins; if they weigh 310g the second bag does, and if they weigh 315g the third bag does.

Answer 16
Sitting Pretty

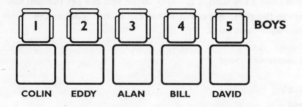

1	2	3	4	5	**BOYS**

COLIN	EDDY	ALAN	BILL	DAVID

HILARY	FIONA	INDIRA	JANE	GRACE

10	9	8	7	6	**GIRLS**

Answer 17
Figure of Fun

C. The number of right angles in each figure increases by one each time.

Answer 18
House Hunting

We have to find the unique number which you can get to from the answers to the three questions. There can be only one, or the question would not work.

1. Is it under 41?

No 41–82
Yes 1-40

2. Is it divisible by 4?

Yes	44	48	52	56	60	64	68	72	76	80	(41-82)
No	41	42	43	45	46	47	49	50	51	53	
	54	55	57	58	59	61	62	63	65	66	
	67	69	70	71	73	74	75	77	78	79	
	81	82									
Yes	4	8	12	16	20	24	28	32	36	40	(1-40)
No	1	2	3	5	6	7	9	10	11	13	
	14	15	17	18	19	21	22	23	25	26	
	27	29	30	31	33	34	35	37	38	39	

3. Is it a square number?

Yes	64 – the unique answer												(41-82, Div 4 OK)
No	44	48	52	56	60	68	72	76	80				
Yes	49	81											(41-82, no Div 4)
No	41	42	43	45	46	47	50	51	53				
	54	55	57	58	59	61	62	63	65	66			
	67	69	70	71	73	74	75	77	78	79	82		
Yes	4	16	36										(1-40, Div 4 OK)
No	8	12	20	24	28	32	40						
Yes	1	9	25										(1-40, no Div 4)
No	2	3	5	6	7	10	11	13					
	14	15	17	18	19	21	22	23					
	26	27	29	30	31	33	34	35	37	38	39		

By answering no to the first question, yes to the second and yes to the third you arrive at the only unique number – 64, which is therefore the number of Archibald's house.

Answer 19
Dynamic Dog

22½ miles. Work out how long it takes Russell Carter to walk home. Spot has been running all this time at his given constant speed, so it is simple to work out how many miles Spot has covered during this period.

Russell walks for 10 miles at 4mph, taking 2½ hours.
Spot is running for 2½ hours too, at 9mph, which means he covers 22½ miles.

Answer 20
Roving Robot

There was a stationary car parked 5m to the robot's right. The program should have said "moving land vehicle".

Answer 21
Dazzling Diamond

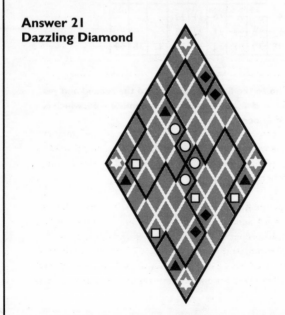

Answer 22
Japan Hotel
"Push" on one side; "Pull" on the other side.

Answer 23
Salary Increase
At first glance the best option seems to be the first. However, the second option works out best.

First option	($500 increase after each 12 months)
First year	$10,000 + $10,000 = $20,000
Second year	$10,250 + $10,250 = $20,500
Third year	$10,500 + $10,500 = $21,000
Fourth year	$10,750 + $10,750 = $21,500

Second option	($125 increase after each 6 months)
First year	$10,000 + $10,125 = $20,125
Second year	$10,250 + $10,375 = $20,625
Third year	$10,500 + $10,625 = $21,125
Fourth year	$10,750 + $10,875 = $21,625

Answer 24
Funny Fingers
Let us assume that 240 fingers could be 20 aliens with 12 fingers each or 12 aliens with 20 fingers each, etc. This does not provide a unique answer so eliminates all numbers that can be factorized (ie non-prime numbers).

Now consider prime numbers: there could be one alien with 229 fingers (not allowed, according to sentence one); or 229 aliens with one finger (not according to sentence two). Simple primes are therefore not allowed, so the rules eliminate all prime numbers – except those squared. There is only one of these between 200 and 300 and that is 289 (17^2). So, in the room there are 17 aliens, each with 17 fingers.

Answer 25
Pick a Pattern
C. The middle pattern is removed and encases the rest of the pattern of the original figure.

Answer 26
Barrels of Fun
The 40-gallon barrel contains beer. The first customer purchases the 30-gallon and 36-gallon barrels, giving 66 gallons of wine. The second customer, therefore, purchases 132 gallons of wine – the 32-gallon, 38-gallon and 62-gallon barrels. The 40-gallon barrel has not been purchased by either customer and therefore contains the beer.

Answer 27
Mouse Moves
As there are 216 chambers – an even number – there is no central chamber. The task is therefore impossible.

Answer 28
Treasured Trees

Tree	Elm	Ash	Beech	Lime	Poplar
Person	Bill	Jim	Tony	Sylvester	Desmond
Club	Squash	Golf	Tennis	Bowling	Soccer
Bird	Owl	Blackbird	Crow	Robin	Starling
Year	1970	1971	1972	1973	1974

Answer 29
Intergalactic Ingenuity
The wife of M9 is F10. The male speaker on nuclear fission is M3.

Male	M1	M3	M5	M9	M7
Female	F8	F6	F4	F10	F2
Vehicle	Warp distorter	Galaxy freighter	Space oscillator	Nebula accelerator	Astro carrier
Speech	Time travel	Nuclear fission	Astral transporting	Mind reading	Anti-gravity
Feature	12 fingers	3 eyes	3 legs	4 arms	Webbed feet

Answer 30
Handkerchief Challenge
Charlie puts the handkerchief under a door and stands on the corner at the other side.

Answer 31
Algarve Rendezvous
On the corner of road 5, street 4. Draw a line down the person who is in the middle on the roads axis. Then draw a line across the person who is in the middle of the streets axis.

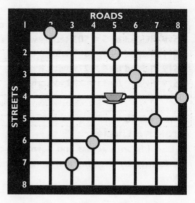

Answer 32
Searching Segments

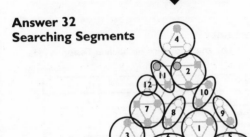

Answer 33
Take a Tile
B. Looking both across and down, any lines common to the first two tiles disappear in the third tile.

Answer 34
Prisoners' Porridge

2,519 prisoners.

2,519 divided by 3 = 839 tables with 2 over
2,519 divided by 5 = 503 tables with 4 over
2,519 divided by 7 = 359 with 6 over
2,519 divided by 9 = 279 with 8 over
2,519 divided by 11 = 229 exactly.

Answer 35
Creative Circles
A. Looking both across and down, the contents of the third square are formed by merging the contents of the two previous squares, as follows:

one white or black circle remains;
two black circles become white;
two white circles become black.

Answer 36
Think of a Number
Anastasia tells a lie when she says that the number is below 500.
The only square and cube between 99 and 999 whose first and last
digit is 5, 7 or 9 is 729.

Answer 37
Dog Delight
The dalmatians are called Andy (owned by Bill) and Donald (owned
by Colin).

Answer 38
Club Conundrum
2. If all 49 women wore glasses then 21 men wore glasses too. If 11
of these men were under 20 years of age, only 10 men older than 20
years of age wore glasses. Then 10 − 8 = 2 men is the minimum
number.

Answer 39
Three Squares

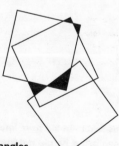

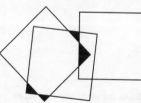

D. The three squares form four triangles.

Answer 40
Roulette Riddle
15.

Answer 41
Tree Teaser
Spencer prunes three more trees than Don.

Answer 42
Girl Talk

The three ages, when multiplied, must be one of the following combinations:	When added, they equal
72 x 1 x 1	74
36 x 2 x 1	39
18 x 4 x 1	23
9 x 4 x 2	15
9 x 8 x 1	18
6 x 6 x 2	14
8 x 3 x 3	14
12 x 6 x 1	19
12 x 3 x 2	17
18 x 2 x 2	22
6 x 3 x 4	13
3 x 24 x 1	28

The census-taker should have known the number of the house, as he could see it, but he did not know their ages, therefore the house must be number 14. He needed more information to decide whether their ages were 6, 6, 2 or 8, 3, 3. When the woman says "eldest" daughter, he knows they were 8, 3, 3.

Answer 43
Lucid Lines

E. The two figures merge into one by superimposing one onto the other. However, when two lines appear in the same position they disappear.

Answer 44
Number Placement
So that:

2	14	10	7
9	6	1	4
16	3	13	11
12	8	5	15

1. No two consecutive numbers appear in any horizontal, vertical or diagonal line;
2. No two consecutive numbers appear in adjacent squares.

Answer 45
Play Watching

D B C A C D A B

C MR

C MRS

187

Answer 46
Suspicious Circles
E. A is a mirror image of C; B is a mirror image of D.

Answer 47
Study Time
Anne studies algebra, history, French and Japanese. Bess studies physics, English, French and Japanese. Candice studies algebra, physics, English and history.

Answer 48
Tricky Triangles
Two segments: all the triangles do not need to be the same size.

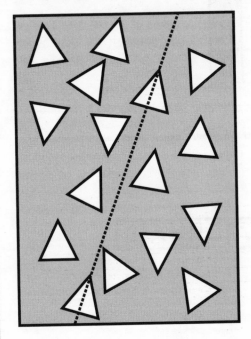

Answer 49
Picking Professions
Mr Carter is the drover.

Answer 50
Great Golfers
Edward Peters; Robert Edwards; Peter Roberts. Mr Peters must be
Edward because the man who spoke last is Robert and he is not Mr
Peters.

Answer 51
Lost Time

11 + 12 + 1 + 2 = 26
10 + 3 + 9 + 4 = 26
5 + 6 + 7 + 8 = 26.

Answer 52
Pleased Pupils

Name	Class	Subject	Sport
Alice	6	Algebra	Squash
Betty	2	Biology	Running
Clara	4	History	Swimming
Doris	3	Geography	Tennis
Elizabeth	5	Chemistry	Basketball

Answer 53
Hello, Sailor

Name	Rank	Ship	Location
Perkins	Steward	Aircraft carrier	Malta
Ward	Seaman	Cruiser	Portsmouth
Manning	Commander	Submarine	Falklands
Dewhurst	Purser	Frigate	Gibraltar
Brand	Captain	Warship	Crete

Answer 54
Gone Fishing

North ◄─────── Pier ───────► South

Name	Joe	Fred	Dick	Henry	Malcolm
Occupation	Banker	Electrician	Professor	Plumber	Salesman
Town	L.A.	Orlando	Tucson	New York	St Louis
Bait	Worms	Bread	Maggots	Shrimps	Meal
Catch	6	15	10	9	1

Answer 55
Winning Wager

It is possible but there has to be a compensating factor. Jim has $8 at the start so Bill can win only $8 even if he wins all 10 frames. Jim, however, can win a large sum if he wins every frame: $8, $12, $18, $27, etc. However, Bill can win a small amount over all, even if he wins two fewer frames than Jim. The order of Jim's winning and losing frames makes no difference to the final total.

Frame	Jim	Jim has $8
1	win	$12.00
2	lose	$6.00
3	lose	$3.00
4	win	$4.50
5	win	$6.75
6	lose	$3.38
7	win	$5.07
8	win	$7.60
9	win	$11.40
10	lose	$5.70 = loses $2.30 from starting $8.00

Answer 56
Odd One Out

E. In all the others, if the line dividing the square is a mirror the correct mirror image has been shown.

Answer 57
Spot the Shape

2A.

Answer 58
Table Talk

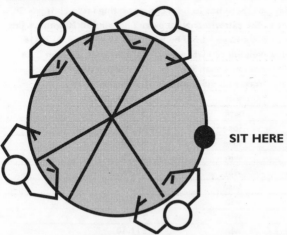

SIT HERE

Mark four points exactly opposite each of the four people. Now count the number of points that lie between each pair. The place to sit is midway between the points. This basic principle can be made to work for any seating plan.

Answer 59
Changing Trains

25 minutes. As the man leaves home according to his normal schedule it is earlier than 6.30pm when he picks up his wife. As the total journey saves 10 minutes, that must be the same time it takes the man from the point he picks up his wife, to the station and back to the same point. Assuming that it takes an equal five minutes each way he has therefore picked up his wife five minutes before he would normally, which means 6.20pm. So his wife must have walked from 6.00pm to 6.25pm, that is for 25 minutes.

Answer 60
Fathers and Daughters

Father	Daughter	Father's age	Daughter's age
John	Alison	52	20
Kevin	Diana	53	19
Len	Betty	50	21
Malcolm	Eve	54	18
Nick	Carol	51	17

Answer 61
Sums about Sons

Graham is 9 years old and Frederick is 27. Thus, 27 squared is the same as 9 cubed = 729. There are 18 steps, 36 palisades and 243 bricks, which, when added together, gives the door number of 297.

Answer 62
Cube Diagonals

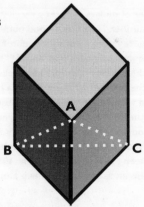

60°. If a third face diagonal, BC, is drawn this completes an equilateral triangle. All its sides are equal because they are cube diagonals. Being equilateral, all its angles are 60°.

Answer 63
Best Beer

18 days. If it takes a man 27 days to drink one barrel, he drinks
0.037 of a barrel each day. Similarly, a woman drinks 0.0185 of
a barrel each day. Added together, a day's combined drinking
consumes 0.0555 of a barrel. In this case, to drink the whole
barrel takes 18.018 days.

Answer 64
Circles and Triangles

C. Each horizontal line and vertical column contains the wavy shape
shown once vertical and once black. Similarly, each line and column
shows the triangle three times: once pointing left, once right, once
down. Other elements are similarly repeated.

Answer 65
Gun Running

$2. The total number of dollars that they receive for their cattle
must be a square number. They buy an odd number of sheep at $10
each, so the tens figure in the total square number must be an odd
number. The only square numbers with an odd "tens"
figure have "6" as their "units" figure. The number 256 is one such
number, equalling the price of 16 steer at $16 a head as well as 25
sheep at $10 a head with $6 for the goat. Because the square number must end in 6, the goat is always worth $6, no matter how
many sheep they bought (16, 36, 256, etc). Bully Bill evens up the
takings by giving Dynamo Dan the goat and Colt .45 to equal his
own share of the sheep ($10) minus the Colt .45. Therefore the gun
is worth half the difference between a sheep and a goat, or $2.

Answer 66
Missing Numbers

The grid should contain one 1, two 2s, three 3s, four 4s, five 5s, six
6s, seven 7s, and eight 8s. Therefore, the missing numbers are 2, 7, 7
and 8. All the numbers are placed so that two identical numbers are
never adjacent.

Answer 67
Rifle Range

Major Mustard. Tabulate the results shown on the board so that each set equals 71. There are only three possible ways to do this given the results: 25, 20, 20, 3, 2, 1; 25, 20, 10, 10, 5, 1; and 50, 10, 5, 3, 2, 1. The first set is Colonel Ketchup's (since 22 cannot be scored in two shots in the other sets); the third set is Major Mustard's (as we know that he scores 3). So, Major Mustard hit the bull's eye.

Answer 68
Round the Hexagons

C. The third hexagon is formed by merging hexagons 1 and 2. The fifth hexagon is formed by merging hexagons 1 and 4. In this way, the hexagons build up the shape along vertical lines going from the bottom hexagon upwards. Continuing this trend, the top hexagon is formed by a merging of hexagons 3, 5, 6, and 7: the two straight lines moving upwards to the top hexagon.

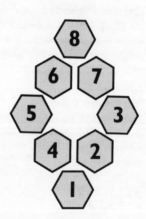

Answer 69
Skyscraper Sizzler

She lives on the 27th floor. The elevator came down from the 36th to the 28th floor – 9 floors; or it came up from the first to the 27th floor – 27 floors. Therefore there is a 3:1 chance of it going up rather than down.

Answer 70
Black and White Balls

Three chances in four. Look at the possible combinations of drawing the balls. There are black–black; white–black; black–white; and white–white. The only one of the four possible combinations in which it does not occur is the fourth one. The chances of drawing at least one black ball are, therefore, three in four.

Answer 71
Carrier Pigeons

No. The pigeons remain at 200lbs even whilst flying. Those flying up would reduce the weight, but those flying down would increase the weight, so balancing the total weight.

Answer 72
Bartender's Beer

The first man places a $1 bill on the counter. The second man puts down three quarters, two dimes and a nickel – amounting to one dollar. Had he wanted a 90-cent beer he had the change to offer the exact amount.

Answer 73
Logical Clocks

A. At each stage, the big hand moves anti-clockwise first by 10 minutes, then 20 and, finally, by 30 minutes (option A). At each stage, the small hand moves clockwise first by one hour, then two hours and, finally, three hours (option A).

Answer 74
Broadway, NY

The fact that the man does not see a door (as in the illustration) indicates that the door must be on the other side – the kerb side. As this is New York, the bus is therefore moving to A.

Answer 75
Water Divining

By lifting the water tank onto its near-side edge.
If you cannot see the far edge then the tank is more
than half full.
If you can just see the far edge then the tank is
exactly half full.
If you can see below the far edge then the tank is less
than half full.

Answer 76
Missing Links

1. In the first bar, 7 x 4 x 8 x 8 x 2 = 3584.
Similarly, 3 x 5 x 8 x 4 = 480, the missing number.
Following the same formula, the missing number in the second bar
is 2268 and in the third, 2688 and 768.
2. In the first bar, 58 x 2 = 116.
In the same vein, 16 x 1 = 16, the missing number. Using the same
formula, the missing number in the second bar is 657 and in the
third, 162 and 72.

Answer 77
City Slicker

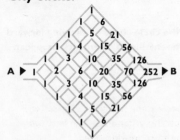

252. Each number represents the cumulative number of possible
routes to each intersection.

Answer 78
Star Gazing

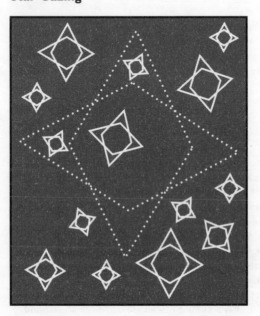

Answer 79
Pyramid Puzzle

D. Each pair of circles produces the circle above by carrying forward only those elements that are different. Similar elements disappear.

Answer 80
Round and Round the Garden

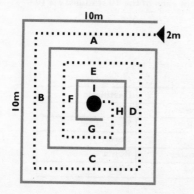

49m. A = 9m B = 8m C = 8m D = 6m E = 6m F = 4m
G = 4m H = 2m I = 2m = TOTAL 49m.

Answer 81
Door Number Puzzle

4-digit numbers made from 1, 4, 6 and 7 will always be divisible by 9 and 3, so the answer is no in both cases, except if the 6 is turned upside down into a 9. If the numbers were 1, 4, 7 and 9, it would never be divisible by 9 but still always divisible by 3.

Answer 82
Dice Dilemma

Number 3.

Answer 83
Triangles and Trapeziums

A. The figures change places so that the one in front goes to the back and vice versa.

Answer 84
Ski-lift
90. You can buy nine tickets from each of the 10 stations: 9 x 10 = 90.

Answer 85
Five Pilots

Name	Airport	Destination
Mike	Heathrow	JFK
Nick	Gatwick	Vancouver
Paul	Cardiff	Berlin
Robin	Manchester	Roma
Tony	Stansted	Nice

Answer 86
Making Moves
J is option 4; N is option 6. The black segments move from top to bottom and right to left in sequence, then rise in the same way. However, when an arrangement has occurred previously it is omitted from the sequence.

Answer 87
Dinner Party Placements
Mr and Mrs Chester.

Answer 88
Careful Calculation
8679. Turn the page upside down and add up the two numbers.

Answer 89
Pyramidal Logic

E. Each symbol is linked to the two below it. No symbol ever appears above an identical one. The symbols are produced as follows:

so that ▦ + ◌ must equal something completely different to anything else in the pyramid. Of the options shown, this can only be: ♧ (E).

Answer 90
Figure Columns

D. The smallest number is dropped each time and the remaining numbers appear in reverse order.

Answer 91
Sunshine

Any valley on or near the equator, owing to the revolution of the Earth.

Answer 92
Shady Squares
C. The square turns 90° clockwise at each stage. Similarly, the shading also moves one segment clockwise at each stage.

Answer 93
Generation Gap
I am 40 and my daughter is 10.

Answer 94
Work it Out
24. In the first circle, 56 + 79 divided by 5 = 27. The same formula applies to circles two and three.

Answer 95
Chess Strategy
Strong, weak, strong. He will always beat the weak player, so playing this way gives him two chances to beat the strong one.

Answer 96
Lonely Loser
E. The others all have rotated symmetry. In other words, if they
were rotated through 180° they would appear exactly the same.

Answer 97
Scratch Card
The number of empty squares on the card is impossible to calcu-
late, and irrelevant to the question. The odds are always 2:1 against.

Answer 98
Frogs and Flies
29.

Answer 99
Lateral Logic
B. There are three sizes of rectangle. In the next three stages A
moves from left to right one stage at a time. Then it is the turn of B
to do the same.

Answer 100
Notable Number
12. The third number, 27, is obtained by adding the digits of the two
preceding numbers – 7 + 2 + 9 + 9. This formula applies throughout
the puzzle.

Answer 101
Pentagon Figures
4. In the first pentagon $5 \times 5 \times 125 = 3125$ or 5^5. In the second
pentagon, $3 \times 9 \times 9 = 243$ or 3^5. In the same way, $16 \times 8 \times 8 = 1024$
or 4^5.

Answer 102
Counting Creatures
44. 28 huskies with four legs each, plus 44 penguins with two each, making 200 in all.

Answer 103
Eighteen Trees

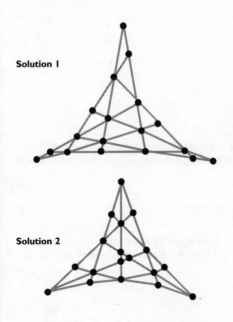

Solution 1

Solution 2

Both solutions produce nine rows of five trees per row.

Answer 104
Fairground Fiesta

Name	Age	Ride	Food
Sam	14	Dodgems	Hot dog
Joe	11	Big dipper	Fries
Don	12	Whirligig	Candy floss
Len	15	Crocodile	Gum
Ron	13	Mountain	Ice cream

Answer 105
Five Circles

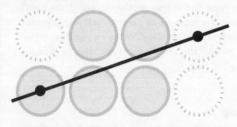

Answer 106
Line Analogy

B. The figures are flipped vertically.

Answer 107
Island Access

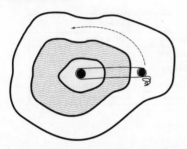

He ties one end of the rope to the tree on the mainland, then walks around the lake carrying the rope. As he reaches half-way, the rope wraps itself around the tree on the island. When he returns to the tree on the mainland, he ties the other end of the rope to it and hauls himself across to the island.

Answer 108
Number Crunching

33. Multiply diagonally opposite squares and subtract the smaller product from the larger:

(13 x 5) - (8 x 4) = 33.

Answer 109
Square Sort

2C.

Answer 110
Round in Circles

C. The striped and black segments are moving in the following sequences: the striped segments move two anti-clockwise then one clockwise in turn, and continue in this way. The black segments move two clockwise then one anti-clockwise in turn, and continue in this way too.

Answer 111
Logic Circles

D. The large white circle moves 180°; the small white circle moves 180°; the black circle moves 90°; and the black dots move 180°.

Answer 112
Easy Equation

$7^2 = 49$. The 6 has been turned over to convert it into a 9 and the 2 becomes a square.

Answer 113
Suspicious Shape

B. A and F are the same, as are C and D, and E and G.

Answer 114
Bird Fanciers

Name	Country	Birds	Collective Noun
Albert	Belgium	Owls	Parliament
Roger	France	Crows	Murder
Harold	Germany	Ravens	Unkindness
Cameron	Scotland	Plovers	Wing
Edward	England	Starlings	Murmuration

Answer 115
Perpetuate the Pattern

F. Column 1 is added to column 2 to make column 3. Similarly, line 1 is added to line 2 to make line 3. In both cases, repeated symbols disappear.

Answer 116
Hexagonal Pyramid

E. The contents of each hexagon are determined by merging the contents of the two hexagons immediately below, except that two identical lines disappear.

Answer 117
Sequence Search

D.

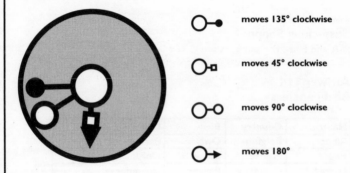

moves 135° clockwise

moves 45° clockwise

moves 90° clockwise

moves 180°

Answer 118
Household Items

First name	Surname	Room	Item
Kylie	Dingle	Conservatory	Computer
Amy	Williams	Bedroom	Television
Clara	Griggs	Living Room	Hi-fi
Roxanne	Simpson	Kitchen	Telephone
Michelle	Pringle	Study	Bookcase

Answer 119
Trying Trominoes
B. There are four different symbols grouped ABC, ABD, BCD and, in answer B, ACD, which completes the set of symbols which are in order and that have one ommission.

A   B   C   D

Answer 120
Pyramid Plot
D. Each pair of circles produces the circle above by carrying on elements that they have in common. Different elements disappear.

Answer 121
Round the Circle
20. Start at 10 and jump to alternate segments, adding 1, then 2, then 3 and so on.

Answer 122
Triangle Teaser

Divide the central number by 5 to give the top number. Add the digits of the central number to give the bottom left number. Reverse the digits of the central number and divide by three to give the bottom right number.

3

15

6

17

Answer 123
Gritty Grid
3A.

Answer 124
Strange Series

If you don't believe this, hold the book up to a mirror. You will see that with the inclusion of the figure on the right, the numbers 1, 2, 3, 4, 5 appear in sequence.

Answer 125
Sticky Business
If the shorter pieces, placed end to end, are longer than the largest piece, then they will form a triangle.

Answer 126
Fancy Figures
Arrange them into groups of three, each totalling 1000.

457 + 168 + 375 = 1000

532 + 217 + 251 = 1000

349 + 218 + 433 = 1000

713 + 106 + 181 = 1000

Answer 127
Unwanted Guest
B. It is a straight-sided figure within a curved figure. The rest are curved figures within a straight-sided one.

Answer 128
Following Fun
D. The small circle moves two on and then one back. The middle-size circle moves one back and then two on. The large circle moves one on and then two back.

Answer 129
Symbol Search
B.

Answer 130
Little and Large
C. B and D, and A and E are the same, with large and small circles reversed.

Answer 131
Terrific Tiling
Turn the page upside down and read off the spaces between the tiles.

Answer 132
Probability Paradox

1:5. There are six possible pairings of the four balls:

1. Red/red
2. Red number 1/white
3. Red number 1/black
4. Red number 2/white
5. Red number 2/black
6. Black/white.

The black/white combination has not been drawn out. This leaves five possible combinations; therefore, the chances that the red/red pairing has been drawn out are 1:5.

Answer 133
Paper Peddling

A D G H F B E C

Answer 134
Drawing Dominoes

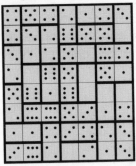

Answer 135
Shapely Sequences

D. Only when a black or white triangle appears three times in the same position in the four surrounding triangles is it transferred to the central circle.

Answer 136
Sweet Sequence

B. There are eight different patterns within the rectangle. Between stages one and two, patterns one and two swap places, then continue to swap at each stage. In stage three patterns three and four start swapping, therefore in stage four patterns five and six start to swap too. Once a pair starts to swap places it continues to swap at each stage.

1	2
3	4
5	6
7	8

Answer 137
Murder Mystery

Ernie Black. The true statements were made by Barry Gloomy, David Dark and Ernie Black.

Answer 138

Coveted Cars

NAME	YEAR	UPHOLSTERY	CAR
CHARLIE	1995	BEIGE	GREEN
JIM	1992	LEATHER	WHITE
BILL	1994	BROWN	BLUE
FRED	1993	TARTAN	BLACK
HARRY	1991	STRIPED	RED

Answer 139
Relative Residences

FIRST NAME	SURNAME	HOUSE NAME	FRONT DOOR
MABEL	STEVENS	ROSE COTTAGE	BLUE
DOROTHY	HILL	HILL HOUSE	RED
GRACE	SULLIVAN	VALLEY VIEW	WHITE
TRACY	PETERS	RIVERSIDE	BLACK
PEGGY	RIVERS	WHITE HOUSE	GREEN
CHERYL	MANBY	CHEZ NOUS	ORANGE

Answer 140
Changing Shape
C. The squares become circles and all segments remain in the same positions, but dark becomes light and vice versa.

Answer 141
Two-tone Teaser
A. Instead of being joined at the top, the two bars are joined at the middle segment. In addition, dark becomes light and vice versa.

Answer 142
Boxing Clever
D. One dot is in a circle only, with the other dot in both a triangle and a square.

Answer 143
Decorative Cards
Numbers 1 and 3. Most people turn 1 and 4 but this is not correct.
1 must be turned; if it has a triangle the answer is yes; if not, it is no.
2 does not need to be turned. If 4 is turned black the answer is yes; if white, it is no. This does not help as it gives no information about 3. Card 3 needs to be turned to see if its other side is black. If it is black the answer is no; if white then it is yes. Therefore 1 and 3 must be turned.

Answer 144
Casino Chips
$27.

Answer 145
Circle Sequence

B. The top circle gets smaller. The bottom curved rectangle gets larger, then starts again. The central circle gets larger. The torpedo shape gets smaller. The right-hand circle alternates in colour.

Answer 146
Creature Comforts

CREATURE	COUNTRY	CHARACTERISTIC	TREASURE
ELF	NORWAY	MALEVOLENT	DIAMONDS
GOBLIN	WALES	REPULSIVE	GOLD
TROLL	SCOTLAND	OBNOXIOUS	RUBIES
LEPRECHAUN	IRELAND	MISCHIEVOUS	EMERALDS
IMP	ENGLAND	UGLY	SILVER

Answer 147
Stocking Search

37: The worst case is all 21 blue, all 14 striped, and 2 black.

Answer 148
Fabulous Football

NAME	TEAM	POSITION	SHIRT
DAVID	GREEN BAY PACKERS	QUARTERBACK	YELLOW
CLAUDE	DALLAS COWBOYS	TACKLE	BLUE
VICTOR	CLEVELAND BROWNS	RUNNING BACK	RED
SAMUEL	OAKLAND RAIDERS	CORNERBACK	BLACK
BILL	CAROLINA PANTHERS	KICKER	PURPLE

Answer 149
Diamond Division

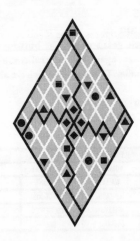

Answer 150
Shapely Search

D. In the example, the two circles become one big circle. The remaining figure – the triangles attached to the arms – then goes inside the large circle. Black figures/lines become pale and vice versa. Similarly, the two squares turn into a large square and from pale to black; the black circles attached to the black arms go inside the square and turn pale.

Working Out

Use the following Notes pages if you need space to work out any of the puzzles.

Notes

Notes

Notes

Notes